SAMUEL RUTHERFORD
AND HIS FRIENDS

SAMUEL RUTHERFORD
AND HIS FRIENDS

Faith Cook

THE BANNER OF TRUTH TRUST

THE BANNER OF TRUTH TRUST
3 Murrayfield Road, Edinburgh EH12 6EL
PO Box 621, Carlisle, Pennsylvania 17073, USA

*

© The Banner of Truth Trust 1992
First published 1992
ISBN 0 85151 635 1

*

Typeset in 10½/12pt Linotron Plantin
At The Spartan Press Ltd,
Lymington, Hants
Printed and bound in Great Britain by
BPCC Hazells Ltd,
Aylesbury, Bucks, England
Member of BPCC Ltd

Contents

ACKNOWLEDGEMENTS

I would like to express my sincere thanks to all who have helped me in the preparation of this book. Most particularly I am indebted to my husband, Paul, for his encouragement, stimulating comment and constructive criticism. A number of friends have kindly read through portions or all of the manuscript and others have assisted in background research. This help has been invaluable. I am especially grateful to the late J. Douglas MacMillan and to Maurice Grant in this respect.

The Evangelical Library in London has often provided timely assistance and I have also received help from the Hornel Library in Broughton House, Kirkcudbright. Lastly, my special thanks are due to Jacky Cogman for the many hours she has given so willingly to typing the manuscript.

I

Samuel Rutherford:
Strong-Winged Eagle

Over three hundred and fifty years have passed since first the small fair-haired pastor of Anwoth in south-west Scotland took up his pen and in his scarcely-legible hand began to write letters to the scattered members of his congregation and to his friends. And yet the letters still live on. Flowing straight from his own deep experience of the Son of God, Samuel Rutherford's words moved, challenged and consoled the hearts of those to whom he wrote. They were read and re-read, then carefully treasured up, and at last in 1664, three years after his death, were gathered together and published.

Since that time the testimony of many to the value of the incomparable *Letters of Samuel Rutherford* has earned for this book a place among the classics of the Christian faith. Charles Haddon Spurgeon, writing in 1891, could exclaim: 'What a wealth of spiritual ravishment we have here! Rutherford is beyond all praise of men. Like a strong-winged eagle he soars into the highest heaven and with unblenched eye he looks into the mystery of love divine.'[1] Through these *Letters* Samuel Rutherford has become a pastor and friend not only to the men and women of his own day but to all who, undaunted by the size of the volume or the quaint phraseology, dip into its pages and find themselves comforted and edified by its soul-stirring words.

*   *   *

Little information has survived concerning Samuel
Rutherford's early years but there is one anecdote that he
himself used to tell. As a child of perhaps five or six years of
age he fell into the village well. His playmates, of course,
rushed to the nearest house with the alarming news that
Sammy had fallen into the well. Moments later, however,
when his would-be rescuers came hurrying to the spot, they
were astonished to find a bedraggled little figure sitting on a
mound of grass not far from the well, soaked to the skin, but
safe. They turned to the lad for an explanation. 'A bonnie
white man came and drew me out of the well', was the simple
reply. This was an experience Samuel Rutherford never
forgot. The precise identity of the 'bonnie white man' may be
unknown but undeniably the God of heaven, seeing the child
in imminent danger, sent from above, took him, and drew
him out of many waters. Samuel Rutherford had a place in
God's plan and his life was precious in His sight. A day was to
come when he was to play a strategic role in the history of the
Christian Church and become a son of consolation to God's
afflicted people through countless generations.

Rutherford's name still excites interest world-wide and a
steady stream of visitors make their way down the winding
lane in rural Anwoth and stand gazing at the roofless ruin of
the old kirk, where he first preached. It is possible to read a
number of biographical sketches of Samuel Rutherford and
his life has been assessed in terms of his contribution as a
theologian, thinker and writer. This present work, however,
is concerned principally with his unique genius as faithful
counsellor and masterly physician of the soul. And for this,
above all, his memory is revered today.

From the scant details we can glean that tell of
Rutherford's younger days it is evident that the circumstances of his early life and experience were ordered by God
that he might be best equipped to understand and counsel
the men and women of his generation. Born in 1600 in the

village of Nisbet, Samuel Rutherford was the son of a fairly prosperous farmer. His father's personal circumstances enabled him to give his three sons – Samuel, George and James – the benefit of an education as complete as the times would allow.

Nisbet lies about four miles from the attractive town of Jedburgh in the Scottish Borders and it is not hard to imagine the brothers playing by the fast-flowing Teviot River or walking to school in Jedburgh each day. The ruins of an old abbey still dominate the town and it is here that the school they attended, known as *Latiner's Alley*, was housed. It was not long before young Samuel's abilities became apparent and his parents decided to make the financial sacrifice necessary to obtain a university education for their son. In 1617 Rutherford became a student at the University of Edinburgh and was awarded a Master of Arts degree in 1621.

Certainly Rutherford's childhood contributed little to his spiritual enlightenment. Nisbet was one of the numerous villages in the land where a man might be born, live out his days and die without any opportunity to hear the gospel of Christ. Writing of his birth-place towards the end of his life, Rutherford expresses the longing that there the wilderness might blossom as the rose, for he says, it was a place 'in which I fear Christ was scarce named'.[2] It caused him much regret that his younger days had been idled away in a godless condition. In a letter to Robert Stuart of Ayr he says, 'Like a fool, as I was, I suffered my sun to be high in the heaven, and near afternoon, before ever I took the gate by the end.'[3]

His own wasted youth gave Rutherford added poignancy when he addressed young people. So he writes to twenty-one-year-old Robert Boyd, whose course all unknown to either of them was swiftly running to its close, 'I beseech your Lordship . . . to cast [your love] in no mould but one, that it may be for Christ only . . . Promise the lodging of your soul first away to Christ . . . And . . . oh, what a sweet couple, what a glorious yoke, are youth and grace, Christ and a young man!'[4]

It was probably not until he was twenty-four years of age that Samuel Rutherford was converted and could write, 'He hath fettered me with His love . . . and left me a chained man.'[5] The strong suggestion that 1624 was the date of his conversion comes in a letter to Robert Gordon of Knockbrex. Writing to his friend in 1638 while banished to Aberdeen for the truth's sake, Rutherford says, 'Christ hath been keeping something these fourteen years for me, that I have now gotten in my heavy days . . . even . . . fresh joys . . . from the fairest face of Christ my Lord.'[6] We learn too from a letter to Lady Busbie that his conversion was not drawn out over many months but rather a swift decisive act of the saving grace of God – 'Oh, but Christ hath a saving eye!' he writes, 'Salvation is in His eyelids! When He first looked on me, I was saved; it cost Him but a look to make hell quit of me!'[7]

*   *   *

In 1627 after two years of theological studies, Rutherford responded to an invitation from Sir John Gordon of Lochinvar – later to become Lord Kenmure – to come to the parish of Anwoth in Galloway. Anwoth had been recently detached from its neighbouring parish of Kirkmabreck and Rutherford was to be its first pastor. So began a ministry lasting only nine years yet one whose fragrance and power has left the name of Anwoth forever stamped on the hearts of Christian people. 'Fair Anwoth by the Solway' became dear above all other places to Samuel Rutherford, but it was not the natural beauty of woods and fields that won for Anwoth so high a place in the preacher's affections; it was the commission he had received from his 'royal and princely Master, my Lord Jesus'[8] to preach Christ to the people. His was the passionate desire of the true pastor for his people's

conversion. 'Oh, if any pain, any sorrow, any loss that I can suffer for Christ, and for you, were laid in pledge to buy Christ's love to you!'[9] he could exclaim. Nor were these mere words, for a contemporary, James Urquhart, minister of Kinloss, records of those days that 'he seemed to be always praying, always preaching, always visiting the sick, always catechising, always writing or studying', and he adds, 'he had two quick eyes, and when he walked it was observed that he held aye his face upwards.'[10] In later years when bereft of his beloved charge, he could write with great pathos, 'Pray for my poor flock . . . I fear that the entering of a hireling upon my labours there will cut off my life with sorrow.' He calls on the woods and hills of Galloway to bear witness to the earnest petitions he had sent heavenward as he strove to 'draw on a fair meeting betwixt Christ and Anwoth'.[11]

At first Rutherford's labours met with little success and he wrote sadly, 'I . . . would be glad to know of one soul to be my crown and rejoicing in the day of Christ.'[12] The people seemed unresponsive and, to add to his despondency, Sir John and Lady Gordon who lived at Rusco Castle only two miles from Anwoth were about to move away. Writing to Lady Jane Gordon, whose spiritual desires had been such an encouragement to the young pastor, he says, 'I have received many and divers dashes and heavy strokes since the Lord called me to the ministry; but indeed I esteem your departure from us amongst the weightiest.'[13]

Yet in spite of the difficulties surrounding the early years in Anwoth, word soon spread throughout the area of the preacher whose power and passion were so intense that Urquhart could also record, 'Many times I thought he would have flown out of the pulpit when he came to speak of Jesus Christ. He was never in his right elements but when he was commending Him. He would have fallen asleep in bed speaking of Christ.'[14] In his *Church History*, Wodrow describes Rutherford as 'one of the most moving and

affectionate preachers in his time or perhaps in any age of the Church'.[15] Many found their steps irresistibly drawn to Anwoth to attend this heart-warming ministry and soon the little church was crowded to capacity.

Communion Sundays were days of special delight and people came from far and near to join the local congregation for these occasions. Marion M'Naught loved to be there. She was the wife of the Provost of Kirkcudbright and a woman of unusual natural abilities, but it was her appreciation of the heart-warming preaching that drew her again and again to near-by Anwoth. Writing to invite her to yet another communion season, Rutherford says, 'I am confident that you shall see the Son of God that day, and I dare in His name invite you to His banquet. Many a time you have been well entertained in His house . . . Yet I speak not this to make you leave off to pray for me, who have nothing of myself.'[16]

Rutherford experienced many personal trials during his early days in Anwoth. Both his children died in infancy and in 1629 his young wife Eupham was taken ill with a distressing and lingering disease. Her sufferings were great: Rutherford describes her condition as one of 'exceeding great torment night and day.'[17] She died after thirteen months of illness, leaving Rutherford bereft, weary and alone; yet it was here in the school of affliction that he learnt to be a compassionate and faithful pastor to Christ's suffering people. In his consolation of the bereaved, Rutherford excels as with sure hand he leads the mourner to the Man of Sorrows and shares the comforts that he himself has known. Writing to one who had recently lost her husband, he says, 'Know, therefore, that the wounds of your Lord Jesus are the wounds of a lover, and that He will have compassion upon a sad-hearted servant . . . He loved you in your first husband's time, and He is but wooing you still. Give Him heart and chair, house and all . . . He will have all your love.'[18]

The old manse at Bush o'Bield and the small copse of trees

separating it from the church have now gone without trace but it is not hard to imagine Samuel Rutherford bowed over his studies by the light of a flickering candle or pacing the tree-lined path earnestly imploring the help of God's Spirit in his preaching. We are told that he often rose at three in the morning to hold communion with his Saviour.

The Anwoth congregation was a widely-scattered one and Rutherford must have spent many hours trudging along upland tracks and through lonely glens to visit his people in their isolated hamlets. It is evident from his letters that he had gained an intimate knowledge of the family circum-stances and spiritual needs of those for whom he had responsibility. His letters are rich in rural allusion and we can imagine that these long 'pastoral' walks were the birth place of much of the graphic imagery that he drew from the world of nature. In a letter to Lady Gaitgirth, he refers to the streams in early spring when the torrents of newly-melted snows come tumbling down the hillside, sweeping away young plants in their downward rush. Turning this to spiritual account, he says, 'He [Christ] knoweth that you could not bear . . . a high spring-tide of His felt love . . . He could not let out His rivers of love upon His own, but these rivers would be in hazard of loosening a young plant at the root; and He knoweth this of you.'[19]

*   *   *

Samuel Rutherford lived in troubled days for the true Church of Jesus Christ. The Reformation, which was nothing less than a great revival of religion, had restored the Word of God to its rightful pre-eminence. Nowhere had this taken place more thoroughly than in Scotland where the powerful preaching of John Knox had written the Reforma-tion truths deeply in the hearts of the people. It is not surprising to find that Rutherford's ministry, following as it did in this same biblical mould, was closely marked by those bishops and clergy anxious to bring the Church back to pre-Reformation forms. Nor could the influence of a man of Rutherford's ability be confined to his quiet country charge. He was in close touch with many other prominent church leaders of his day and joined them in resisting any change that undermined biblical truth.

When the arrogant and intolerant Thomas Sydserff became Bishop of Galloway in 1634, Rutherford knew that his ministry was threatened. Writing to Lady Kenmure (a title she assumed when Sir John became Viscount of Kenmure in 1633), he referred to the darkening situation. 'I expect our new prelate shall try my sitting. I hang by a thread, but it is (if I may speak so) of Christ's spinning.'[20] Early in 1636, Rutherford published a book which exposed with devastating clarity the Arminian errors of Archbishop Laud, Charles 1's right-hand man.[21] His fate was sealed. He faced an ecclesiastical court in Wigtown summoned by Bishop Sydserff, a sycophant of Laud, and this was followed by a further farcical trial in Edinburgh in July 1636. The case against him was so flimsy that apart from the intransigence of Sydserff, it would have been dismissed. But in spite of the intervention of Lady Kenmure's brother, the Lord of Lorn (later to become Marquis of Argyll), Rutherford was sentenced to banishment in Aberdeen and prohibited from any further preaching.

Rutherford's immediate reaction was one of joy at the privilege of suffering for Christ's sake. But he was under no illusions. He knew that these were but the early rumblings of a storm that was to break out with horrifying ferocity in days to come. 'I apprehend no less than a judgment upon Galloway, and that the Lord shall visit this whole nation for the quarrel of the Covenant,' he predicts in a letter to Lady Kenmure.[22] Although he grieved over the prospect of leaving his little flock pastorless, the full weight of the loss

[8]

with all its implications was mercifully hidden from him at this stage. It was not until the early months of his banishment that he struggled against so heavy an affliction and felt the whole burden of the separation.

So began twenty-two months of banishment from home and friends: a period when the preacher was forbidden by his enemies to proclaim the truths he loved. But like John Bunyan, who made his noblest and most lasting contribution to the Church of Jesus Christ during his period of imprisonment for the gospel's sake, so too Rutherford now took up his pen and began to write: not the penetrating and moving sermons of the tinker of Bedford, but over two hundred inimitable letters to his Anwoth parishioners and scattered friends.

Rutherford wrote straight from his heart to the needs of others. These letters were never intended for the public eye: they were not polished or revised and sometimes words seemed to tumble over each other and compete with each other to give expression to the passionate and exalted thoughts of his mind. At times he may have transgressed the bounds of discretion in his rapturous expressions of adoration, for his was the mind and heart of the poet. But to press his metaphors to their logical extreme is to do him an injustice.

During the early months of his banishment in Aberdeen as he sat alone in his room at No.44, Upper Kirkgate, Rutherford's sufferings were intensified by the great 'Accuser of the brethren' who insinuated to the exiled pastor that God had dispensed with his services because of spiritual failure. He felt cast off and useless. Bereaved of wife and children, his preaching had been his 'poor man's one eye' and now he cried out in desolation of spirit, 'That day that my mouth was must unjustly and cruelly closed, the bloom fell off my branches, and my joy did cast the flower . . . I dare not say that the Lord hath put out my candle, and hath casten water upon my poor coal . . . but I have tasted bitterness, and eaten gall and wormwood since that day on which my Master laid bonds upon me to speak no more.'[23]

Above all, it was his 'dumb Sabbaths' that distressed the pastor from Anwoth. Writing to Alexander Gordon, a man of Galloway who had known much persecution for his stand for truth, Rutherford complains, 'At first the remembrance of the many fair feast-days with my Lord Jesus in public, which are now changed into silent Sabbaths, raised a great tempest in my soul. The devil came in, and would prompt me to make a plea with Christ, and lay the blame on Him as a hard master.'[24]

The remembrance of his Anwoth flock, now left as 'sheep without a shepherd', caused him many a troubled thought. Unable to exhort them in person, he wrote long pastoral letters: 'I long exceedingly to know if the oft-spoken-of match betwixt you and Christ holdeth, and if ye follow on to know the Lord. My day-thoughts and my night-thoughts are of you: while ye sleep I am afraid of your souls . . . '[25] Robbed of his pulpit, he must take up his pen, for some were in danger of backsliding, others had been bereaved and still others were sorely perplexed at God's dealings with them. Letters of rebuke, warning, comfort and instruction were addressed to each according to the individual need.

If Rutherford's trials were great, so were his consolations and a predominant note in all the Aberdeen letters is one of exultant praise at the kindness of God to a poor prisoner. To Robert Gordon of Knockbrex he is able to say, 'How blind are my adversaries, who sent me to a banqueting-house, to a house of wine, to the lovely feasts of my lovely Lord Jesus, and not to a prison, or place of exile!'[26] and when he writes to Alexander Gordon of Knockgray, he strains language to its utmost limits in his search for words to express the blessings he knows. 'Faith may dance because Christ singeth; and we may . . . shout for joy with our Lord Jesus . . . Christ and

His cross together are sweet company, and a blessed couple. My prison is my palace, my sorrow is with child of joy, my losses are rich losses, my pain easy pain.'[27]

The secret of this joy lay in the extraordinary measures of the love of Christ that God granted to His servant at this time. We only wonder at his exotic language because we are largely unacquainted with his joys. It was heaven on earth to Samuel Rutherford and only language akin to that of the Song of Solomon could suffice to give expression to it. Writing to John Nevay, Rutherford confides, 'I would desire no more for my heaven beneath the moon, while I am sighing in this house of clay, but daily renewed feasts of love with Christ . . . I find that it is possible to find young glory, and a young green paradise of joy, even here.'[28]

These manifestations of the love of God were by no means an end in themselves but led directly to heightened affections for the Son of God. The dominant theme of all these letters is the majesty and loveliness of the person of Christ. Here all the passion and poetry latent in Rutherford's soul spring to life as he describes his well-beloved Saviour. 'Oh, what a fair One, what an only One, what an excellent, lovely, ravishing One, is Jesus! Put the beauty of ten thousand thousand worlds of paradises, like the Garden of Eden in one . . . it would be less to that fair and dearest Well-beloved, Christ.'[29]

*   *   *

During Rutherford's period of exile thirteen letters were carried by 'bearers' who happened to be making the journey to Galloway to the seclusion of Kenmure Castle where Lady Jane Kenmure had lived since her return from London with her husband in 1633. She had received some of the earliest letters from his pen and the entire correspondence preserved to us numbers over forty letters. These date from 1628 until shortly before Rutherford's death in 1661. Some were letters of compassion, for Lady Kenmure experienced constant affliction, others were of encouragement and Christian fellowship.

During Rutherford's Anwoth days Lady Kenmure was bereaved of her three infant daughters. Following the death of each child Rutherford wrote letters of sympathy – letters which not only brought comfort to Lady Kenmure but which have also strengthened countless Christians in subsequent generations. 'I believe faith will teach you to kiss a striking Lord . . . If our dear Lord pluck up one of His roses who can challenge Him? . . . Let the movables go; why not? They are not yours. Fasten your grips upon the heritage; and our Lord Jesus give your Ladyship to grow as a palm-tree on God's Mount Zion; howbeit shaken with winds, yet the root is fast.'[30]

In 1634 Lady Kenmure sustained further bereavement when her husband, Sir John, also died and at only thirty-five years of age. Sir John had caused his pastor frequent anxiety because of his careless disregard of spiritual values in his pursuit of worldly honours. But Rutherford attended him as he lay dying at Kenmure Castle and through his words Sir John was brought to repentance. The conversations that took place at that time were recorded by Rutherford himself and published in 1649 under the title *The Last and Heavenly Speeches and Glorious Departure of John, Viscount Kenmure*. The account is unique and moving, for Sir John in his dying was granted the privilege of glorifying the God he had neglected, as he laid hold on His grace and fled at last to Christ for mercy and forgiveness.

Shortly after the death of her husband, Lady Kenmure gave birth to a son, also called John. Rutherford took the concerns of Lady Kenmure and her infant son very much to heart and in almost every letter from Aberdeen he asks after the welfare of her child. 'I cannot forget your Ladyship and that sweet child,' he would write. When the boy died at the age of four, Rutherford shared her grief and was quick to write: 'Madam, I would that I could divide sorrow with you, for your ease. But I am but a beholder . . . the God of comfort speak to you, and allure you with His feasts of love.' There is solace in Christ for the suffering child of God and Rutherford was anxious to point this out: 'I shall believe, for my part, that He mindeth to distil heaven out of this loss . . . for wisdom devised it, and love laid it on, and Christ owneth it as His own and putteth your shoulder beneath only a piece of it.' Only a meek acceptance of the purposes of God can bring peace to the heart and this Rutherford urges on his bereaved friend: 'Madam, subscribe to the Almighty's will; put your hand to the pen, and let the cross of your Lord Jesus have your submissive and resolute AMEN.'[31] It is little wonder that Lady Kenmure treasured up such a letter.

A wide circle of other men and women drawn from all classes of society were also privileged to receive letters from the banished pastor. Lady Boyd, whose Christian zeal and support of the work of God had become a by-word, and Marion M'Naught of Kirkcudbright both received penetrating and memorable letters from his pen. But it was not only to the distinguished that Rutherford wrote: many young Christians were numbered among his correspondents. William Gordon of Earlston, one day to seal his testimony with his blood, was scarcely more than a teenager but four letters were directed to this young man. Marion M'Naught's daughter, Grizzel, was not forgotten, nor were Lady Boyd's sons. The spiritual condition of old John Gordon of Cardoness Castle weighed heavily on Rutherford's heart and eight letters were directed to him and to his family.

Throughout these letters we are granted a window into Rutherford's very soul. We share his griefs, we marvel at his joys, and we track the dealings of God with His servant as he passes from distress and turbulence of spirit to a calm resignation of mind and heart in the ways of God. One short letter written to Isabella Macadam seems to mark this spiritual transition: 'There is no great reckoning to be made of the withering of my flower . . . Nay . . . let the bloom fall from my joy, and let it wither, let the Almighty blow out my candle, so being the Lord might be great . . . and His oppressed church delivered.'[32]

Rutherford had a life-view that stands in stark contrast to the materialism of our own day. He saw this life predominantly as a school or training ground where Christ's children were prepared for their lasting home. Writing to Jean Brown, mother of the able expositor John Brown of Wamphray, he says, 'Happy are they who have passed their hard and wearisome time of apprenticeship, and are now freemen and citizens in that joyful, high city, the New Jerusalem;'[33] and to Lady Robertland, 'We are still ill-scholars, and will go in at heaven's gates wanting the half of our lesson.'[34]

Above all else Rutherford viewed this life from the perspective of eternity. He longed for 'Immanuel's Land' and sometimes seemed scarcely able to tolerate the slow march of time. 'O sweet Lord Jesus,' he exclaims, 'take wide steps! O my Lord, come over mountains at one stride! . . . Oh, if He would fold the heavens together like an old cloak, and shovel time and days out of the way, and make ready in haste the Lamb's wife for her Husband!'[35]

Sometimes it seems that the blessings of the world to come were so desirable in Rutherford's eyes that even death itself took on a gilded aspect as the gateway into this indescribable bliss. In a letter to a bereaved mother, he can say, 'O happy and blessed death, that golden bridge laid over by Christ my Lord, between time's clay-banks and heaven's shore!'[36] To Rutherford's soaring imagination, death had not only lost its sting but had become a welcome friend. The greatest solace he could offer the bereaved was the certainty of joys that could not be snatched away by the pitiless passage of years.

[14]

'Build your nest upon no tree here,' he counselled Lady Kenmure when she lost her first little daughter in death, 'for ye see God hath sold the forest to death; and every tree whereupon we would rest is ready to be cut down . . . therefore sigh and long for the dawning of that morning . . . when the shadows shall flee away.'[37]

*   *   *

During the long months of Samuel Rutherford's Aberdeen confinement the tension between Church and State was steadily rising. Charles I was astute enough to know that unless he could lay a heavy hand on Scottish Church affairs, his hold over his northern kingdom could be only tenuous. His strategy lay in the steady strengthening of the episcopal system at the expense of Presbyterianism and the master-mind behind his endeavours was that of Archbishop Laud.

Matters came to a head in 1637 when Charles tried to enforce the Five Articles of Perth introduced in his father's reign. These Articles brought many practices into Church worship strongly reminiscent of pre-Reformation days and were alien to the conscience of the majority of the Scottish people. At last, when Charles commanded that Laud's new liturgy be brought into regular use, the situation erupted. On July 23, 1637, the atmosphere at St Giles in Edinburgh was charged with tension as the Dean, James Hannay, rose to conduct worship from the new prayer book. It was Jenny Geddes and her proverbial reaction, throwing her stool at the Dean's head, that provided the occasion for resentment to boil over into riot. The traditional spot, so near to the unfortunate Dean that she could scarcely miss, can still be seen.

By the end of February 1638, the Presbyterian Church was ready with its answer to the King and what more fitting reaction than a National Covenant? The Scots were a covenanting people: the signing of personal declarations of intent in their spiritual lives and at a church level was deeply ingrained in their religious thought since the Reformation truths had emancipated the people from the shackles of Rome. Previous covenants had been sworn but the National Covenant of 1638, based on the King's Confession of 1581, superseded all others. It profoundly affected Church and nation, giving birth to the concept of the covenanting Church of Jesus Christ, and was the reference point for much of the heroism and endurance that marked the rest of the century.

The architects of the 1638 Covenant were Alexander Henderson, a man risen from relative obscurity to serve his Church in her hour of need, and Archibald Johnston of Warriston. It is not hard to imagine the scene in Greyfriars Church, Edinburgh, as the terms of the Covenant, repudiating popery and alien modes of worship and confirming Reformation principles, were solemnly read out to a tense and packed congregation. For many hours the great deerskin was signed within the church, continuing on into the night long after darkness had shrouded the historic scene. Deep emotions were displayed as the Covenant was etched with the signatures of earnest men and women. Copies were made and carried throughout the length and breadth of the land. The people rose up as one man to sign the Covenant; some wrote, 'until death' after their names, little knowing what bloodshed awaited the Church before religious freedom was finally granted.

Was Samuel Rutherford present on this momentous occasion? Some have said he was. The artist W. Hole, in his well-known picture depicting the scene, shows Rutherford watching with clasped hands as Lord Rothes signs the Covenant. Even Lady Kenmure is drawn standing close by. Andrew Thomson, in his excellent biographical sketch of the great Covenanter first published in 1884, follows this line, as do other biographers. He reports that Rutherford, appar-

moving from Anwoth. Also, Rutherford played a prominent part in the decisions made in the General Assemblies of the Church.

It was in 1640, after five months in St Andrews, that Rutherford, who had been a widower for ten years, married Jean McMath. A glowing testimony of this woman has survived from early records and from this we learn that she was a woman of known spiritual worth.

*   *   *

In 1643 came the signing of the Solemn League and Covenant between England and Scotland at an hour when the Parliamentary cause in the Civil War had sunk to its lowest ebb. Parliament desperately needed the military strength of the Scots in its struggle against the Royalists but the price for such assistance was distinctly ecclesiastical. Under the terms of the Solemn League and Covenant its adherents pledged to promote a uniformity in confessions of faith, church government and order of worship between the English Church and its northern neighbour. Following this event, an Assembly of Divines was convened whose main function would be to hammer out a careful and definitive statement of faith and practice on behalf of both churches. So began the famous Westminster Assembly, whose four years of intensive work produced the Confessions of Faith, Directory of Worship and Catechisms that have become the reference point for reformed theology in succeeding generations.

Once again Samuel Rutherford's gifts were called upon in the service of his Church and he was appointed as one of the four main Scottish representatives to go to London and engage upon this task. Side by side with the most gifted and godly English divines, Rutherford, Robert Baillie, Alexander Henderson and young George Gillespie were to labour on the momentous undertaking. So it was that on November 20, 1643, Rutherford arrived in the English capital after a hazardous voyage down the east coast.

Although known to posterity world-wide by his *Letters*, to Rutherford himself these four years in London represented the most conscious and deliberate contribution of his entire life to the work of God. He flung himself into it with characteristic intensity and with all the zeal of a purist laboured to see the Presbyterian system of church order established in the English Church, replacing the episcopal hierarchy that had so threatened true religion in Scotland.

To set forth his convictions, three weighty tomes came from Rutherford's pen in the 1640s. He was not striving merely to present a credible case for one theory of church government. To him the glory of Christ Himself was intrinsically bound up with the nature and worship of His Church in its purity and power. So volume after volume was submitted in defence of Presbyterian polity.

A Peaceable and Temperate Plea for Paul's Presbytery in Scotland was the first of the trilogy. Published in 1642 and generally acclaimed as the most dispassionate and restrained of the three, it has now become a volume difficult to obtain. In its pages Rutherford argues cogently for the rule of the Church according to a Presbyterian discipline, basing his argument on injunctions from both Christ and the apostles. The *Due Right of Presbyteries; or, a Peaceable Plea for the Government of the Church of Scotland* followed two years later when John Robinson and the New England Independents were singled out for special attention. It also dealt largely with questions of authority and discipline within the Church. Finally in 1646 came the *Divine Right of Church Government and Excommunication* in which Rutherford drew out his sword to thrust at disputants, particularly those of an episcopal persuasion.

In the context of the Westminster Assembly all

Rutherford's abilities as thinker, debater and theologian came into play. He was among the most active of the one hundred and fifty-one members present and remained at the work longer than most. He was one of the final committee of four appointed in October 1647 to complete the Shorter Catechism. In Edinburgh University library a catechism written in Rutherford's own distinctive hand may still be seen. The quaint, graphic and metaphorical expressions mark it out unmistakably as his work. From its similarity in content, though not in style, to the Westminster Assembly's own Shorter Catechism it has been inferred that Rutherford was one of the principal contributors to that important document.

Controversy was inevitable at such a gathering, including as it did men of exceptional ability but drawn together from widely-differing backgrounds and viewpoints. Although among the foremost in voicing his opinions and often puzzled by the theological stance of some good men, Rutherford was not soured by disputes and was generous in his praise of those with whom he differed. 'I judge that in England the Lord hath many names and a fair company, that shall stand at the side of Christ, when He shall render up the Kingdom to the Father; and that in that renowned nation there be men of all ranks, wise, valorous, generous . . . gracious, learned.'[42]

During his period in London, Rutherford and his wife suffered the loss of their two young children. He wrote sorrowfully of this to another bereaved parent, 'I had but two children, and both are dead since I came hither . . . The good Husbandman may pluck His roses, and gather in His lilies at mid-summer, and, for aught I dare say, in the beginning of the first summer month.'[43] News from home was intermittent, for communications were slow and it was during this period that his correspondent Lady Boyd died. The Civil War had raged its weary and destructive way across the land and with the defeat of the King in 1646, tension was mounting between the army and Parliament as to the future settlement of the kingdom. So it was with relief that Rutherford turned his face homeward once more and on November 9, 1647, nearly four years to the day, left the capital for the bracing air of home.

*   *   *

The remaining fourteen years of Rutherford's life were spent at St Andrews, although other institutes of learning earnestly solicited his services. On his return he was made Principal of St Mary's College; his initials, together with those of Andrew Melville, may still be seen high up on the College wall unnoticed by the busy passer-by. In 1651 he was to become Rector of St Andrews University. In spite of a heavy schedule of lecturing and preaching, Rutherford still found time to write. A far-sighted treatise, *A Survey of the Spiritual Antichrist*, published in 1648, dealt in masterly fashion with Antinomianism, a heresy rife in his day and recurring in varied forms ever since. Throughout these years he laboured on another work near to his heart; this was a commentary on the Book of Isaiah but regrettably that manuscript was lost at the Restoration in 1660.

It was during the 1650s that Samuel Rutherford became deeply involved in the sad dissension of the Resolutioners and Protesters that tore the Scottish Church apart for many years. This was a controversy which originated with an attempt on the part of certain of the Scottish nobles to come to an understanding with Charles 1. In return for assurances that the King would uphold the Solemn League and Covenant, and establish Presbyterianism in both realms for at least a trial period, they raised an army on his behalf but were soundly beaten by Cromwell at Preston.

A powerful section of the Scottish nation had opposed any such negotiation with the King, deeply distrusting his reliability. After this defeat, legislation was passed known as the Act of Classes, so called because it divided those involved with Charles I into 'classes' according to their degree of disaffection from the Covenant. It prohibited many of Charles' supporters from taking any further civil or military office. In 1650 the Scottish army rose again, this time in support of their young king-designate, shortly to become Charles II. Heedless of Cromwell's entreaties and with depleted forces, they fought, but suffered serious defeat at Dunbar.

Many in the nation then felt that the discriminating legislation would have to be repealed if they were to have any hope of defending their newly-crowned King against the military might of Oliver Cromwell. For such a step it was considered vital to gain the approval of the General Assembly, but this was not easily obtained. Many members of the Assembly were justly suspicious of the sincerity of Charles II, although he had recently sworn to uphold the Covenants at his coronation in Scone on January 1, 1651. Eventually in July of that year, certain Public Resolutions were passed permitting all but the most notorious 'malignants' (or enemies of the Covenant) back into office. No sooner was this done than Parliament moved to rescind the Act of Classes, but ignored the qualification passed by the Assembly. Some Church leaders, however, were seriously disturbed that these Resolutions had been passed at all and tabled a 'Protest' against them, fearing that the Covenant itself and Reformation principles were at stake. They were right. Godless and unprincipled men, re-admitted to power at this time, were later to become relentless persecutors of the Covenanters. Prominent among these were the Earl of Middleton, the Duke of Lauderdale and the Duke of Hamilton.

Good men were to be found on both sides of the divide, though the majority were Resolutioners. Rutherford's friends David Dickson and James Wood were among them, while Rutherford, with all the vehemence of his intense nature, was a Protester. Bitter and hurtful things were said and written, especially by Rutherford, and in some ways these years form a sad interlude in the life of so great a man. Wounds were healed and friendships restored before Rutherford's death, but the effect of controversy undoubtedly marred his spiritual joy. The letters that came from Rutherford's pen at this time bear the scars of controversy and reveal only occasional flashes of the depth and beauty of some of his earlier correspondence. Writing to Lady Kenmure of these things, he says, 'We are now shouldering and casting down one another in the dark, and the godly are hidden from the godly;'[44] and in another letter, 'There is an universal complaint of deadness of spirit on all that know God. He that writeth to you, Madam, is as deep in this as any.'[45]

A contemporary comment bears this out. The Laird of Glanderston records: 'One day when preaching in Edinburgh, after dwelling for some time on the differences of the day, he (Rutherford) broke out with – "Woe is unto us for these sad divisions, that make us lose the fair scent of the Rose of Sharon!" and then he went on commending Christ, going over all his precious styles and titles about a quarter of an hour.' The Laird could contain himself no longer, saying in a loud whisper, 'Ay, now you are right – hold you there.'[46]

Allowances must be made for the Resolutioners who acted in the light of the military necessity of the situation, but as Thomas McCrie points out, 'It is not difficult for us who have the light of subsequent history to see that the Protesters "had their eyes open while the Resolutioners were blind".'[47] Nor were Rutherford and his fellow Protesters insisting that all who held positions of authority should be converted men: 'We are not for an army of saints, and free from all mixture of ill–affected men,' he maintained in his *Testimony to the*

Covenanted Work of Reformation, written shortly before his death.[48]

Much has been written concerning the paradox of the supposed dual personality to be found in the nature of Samuel Rutherford. By his own confession he was a man 'made of extremes', and these extremes found their most dramatic expression in the contrasts revealed in the one who could write stern, dry and polemical treatises on the one hand, engaging in intense and sometimes bitter invective in pursuit of his argument, and on the other the tender and saintly pastor who could touch the deepest sensitivities of the human heart in consolation and encouragement. A. Taylor Innes, in an otherwise masterly article on Samuel Rutherford, comes to the conclusion that here we have two natures in one man that were never fused into one strong unit; these contrasts, maintains Taylor Innes, were in fact the outward sign of an inward schism of personality: 'That inward schism is strong and startling. It looks sometimes as if there were two men in him. One was the man whom all know in his letters – ardent, aspiring, and unworldly . . . rapt into the continual contemplation of one unseen Face, finding . . . his happiness in its returning smile. The other man was the intellectual gladiator, the rejoicing and remorseless logician, the divider of words . . . the incessant and determined disputant.'[49] Alexander Whyte, popular preacher, writer and Moderator of the Free Church Assembly, accepts Taylor Innes' thesis wholeheartedly and describes his work as 'the finest thing that has ever been written on Rutherford',[50] but this, in common with many of Whyte's conclusions on Rutherford, is wide of the mark. Whyte's own inward and spiritual conflicts often colour his assessment of his heroes.

It would surely be more helpful to follow Robert Gilmour's excellent analysis of Rutherford's nature in his biography on the great Covenanter, with which Sir Marcus Loane in *Makers of Puritan History* entirely concurs: 'That

SAMUEL RUTHERFORD AND HIS FRIENDS

there were two men in Rutherford is most true, but it is only
true in the sense that logical and mystical tendencies may be
said to exist more or less in every one of us. It is in great
minds like that of Rutherford where the very intensity of the
nature forces the different tendencies into sharp contradic-
tion that the so-called problem appears. We need not quarrel
with the kindly providence that has given the Church of
Scotland in the person of a stern and rugged Covenanter, her
greatest scholastic and her greatest mystic in one.'[51]

*   *   *

A day was soon to come when the troubles of the people of
God in both kingdoms were to break out in fearsome
intensity but the Lord spared Rutherford's sensitive spirit
from witnessing such horror. By the mid-1650s it was clear
that he was an ill man. As early as 1653 he had referred in a
letter to Lady Kenmure to 'warnings of my removal'[52] and
by 1657 he complained of a 'craziness of body', that
prevented him from moving from place to place and
described himself as 'a piece of sickly clay'.[53] By 1659 he was
clearly frailer and at one point his life was despaired of. 'I was
lately knocking at death's gate,' he tells Lady Kenmure, 'yet
could I not get in, but was sent back for a time.'[54]

In 1660 Charles II was restored to his throne and only then
did all the malice and deceit of his renegade nature fully
manifest itself, to the bewilderment of many of his loyal
Scottish subjects. This was their King who had, with
apparent sincerity, added his signature to the Solemn League
and Covenant in 1650, and promised to uphold Presbyterianism; yet now his total volte-face on all his declarations
revealed his true disposition.

Vengeance was in the heart of the King for the years of
forced submission to the spiritual ideals of his northern
subjects. Some of Scotland's most distirguished citizens

were singled out for destruction and the Marquis of Argyll, Lady Kenmure's brother, was the first to suffer. It was he who had placed the crown on the head of young Charles in 1651 and his pathetic loyalty to his King hid from his sight the danger signals that others could observe. As soon as he travelled south to congratulate the returning monarch, he was summarily imprisoned in the Tower of London, only to emerge a condemned man, to face the executioner's block in May 1661.

James Guthrie, whose loyalty was beyond question, was the next to die because he refused to allow his King absolute authority in Christ's Church. Archibald Johnston gained only temporary respite on the Continent before the King's spies tracked him down and he too faced a harrowing death on the gallows in 1663.

Samuel Rutherford was a marked man. In 1644 he had published his controversial book *Lex Rex* or *The Law and the Prince*, which had excited great public attention. The country was embroiled in the Civil War at the time and in that war Rutherford fought not with sword but with pen. In this far-sighted treatise he argued closely and powerfully against the arbitrary and tyrannical rule of the monarch. Absolute power belonged to God alone and was a fit garland only for the King of kings. Although he strongly advocated the obedience and loyalty of a subject to his ruler, yet a king who perverted justice and oppressed the rights of his people must be restrained, and in certain extreme cases could forfeit his right to kingship. *Lex Rex* has been described as one of the ablest pleas in defence of a constitutional and democratic government.[55] The concepts behind *Lex Rex* were not original to Rutherford. Clearly he followed John Knox in these views when with devastating argument Knox had silenced the petulant Mary, Queen of Scots,[56] but such writing was inflammatory. The book was condemned as treasonable by the Committee of Estates and copies were publicly burnt outside his window at St Mary's College in St Andrews and in Edinburgh. Not content with outlawing the work, Charles II must now also destroy its author.

When the King's emissaries arrived bearing the summons for his arrest on charges of treason, Samuel Rutherford was already dying. 'Tell them', he said, with a fearlessness born of long submission to a greater King, 'that I have a summons already from a superior Judge and judicatory and I behove to answer my first summons. Ere your day arrives I shall be where few kings and great folks come.'[57] Samuel Rutherford died well. Long years before, he had exhorted John Kennedy of Ayr to prepare his heart for death whenever the last enemy should strike. 'Have all in readiness against the time that ye must sail through that black and impetuous Jordan . . . The last tide will not wait you one moment . . . ',[58] he had written. Death held no terrors for Rutherford; rather it rendered him service, for it ushered him into the joys he had so long anticipated. 'I grant that death is . . . a very new thing,' he wrote when Lady Boyd died, 'but heaven was prepared of old',[59] and only then would there be eternal recompense for all the sorrows of this life. 'Wait with the wearied night watch for the breaking of the eastern sky, and think that ye have not a tomorrow,'[60] he urged young Lady Kenmure before she had attained her thirtieth birthday; and to Jean Brown he wrote, 'Oh! then let us pull up the stakes . . . of our tent, and take our tent on our back, and go . . . to our best home, for here we have no continuing city.'[61]

Rutherford lived to see all he had striven for over thirty years crumbling before his eyes. An ideal Church both in order and worship had been his vision, but the enemies of the Covenant, with all the authority of Charles II behind them, trampled ruthlessly on the labour of many decades; and the Drunken Parliament of 1661, as it was called, gleefully rescinded each act on the statute book that safeguarded Reformation principles.

The day before his death the Act Rescissory made every Parliamentary Act since 1640 null and void. Like Knox before him who said on his death-bed, 'Call for me, dear brethren, that God in His mercy will please to put an end to my long and painful battle . . . For as the world is weary of me, so am I of it,'[62] Rutherford, too, died 'not having received the promises, but having seen them afar off'. But he died in faith and his true life ideal was not denied him, for in his dying he was granted an experience of Christ that fulfilled the desire of years. 'A borrowed vision in this life would be my borrowed and begun heaven,'[63] he once wrote, and this was his portion during those last weeks of life.

Samuel Rutherford has been called 'the Saint of the Covenant'. This is a twentieth century description, but even in his own day, some of those most virulently opposed to his views were compelled to acknowledge, however grudgingly, the quality of his walk with God. Maddened with hate, the 'Drunken Parliament' voted that Rutherford should not be allowed to die in his College. 'Ye have voted that honest man out of the College,' protested Lord Burleigh, 'but ye cannot vote him out of heaven.' 'Hell is too good for him,' came the warped reply, to which Lord Burleigh answered, 'I wish I were as sure of heaven as he is, I should think myself happy to get a grip of his sleeve to haul me in.'[64]

Many watched round that death-bed in St Andrews, eager to catch the last sayings of a man whose eyes at times seemed to pierce through the skies and see that One 'whose face was more and more his Universe.'[65] Nor were they disappointed; but Rutherford himself saw all his spiritual attainments as worthless to redeem the soul. When reminded of his service to God, he could say, 'I disclaim all. The port that I would be in at is redemption and salvation through His blood.'[66]

Through many years Rutherford had longed to 'dwell in Immanuel's high and blessed land'. 'What do we here but sin and suffer?' he would cry, and then add with strong desire,

'Oh, when shall the night be gone, the shadows flee away, and the morning of that long, long day, without cloud or night, dawn?'[67] Now he stood on the very borders of that land. His sensitive ear seemed to catch the strains of heavenly music and repeatedly he was heard to call out, 'Oh for a well-tuned harp!' as though on tip-toe of longing, eager to join the anthems of praise above.

Among those who stood around his bed was one little girl of eleven years of age. It was Agnes, Rutherford's only surviving child out of the seven borne to him by his second wife, Jean. As he looked at his young daughter, he said, 'I have left her upon the Lord.' Recovering from a period of unconsciousness on the last day of his life, he declared, 'I feel, I feel, I believe, I joy and rejoice, I feed on manna.' And then to Robert Blair, who stood near, he murmured, 'Mine eyes shall see my Redeemer . . . and I shall be ever with Him . . . O, for arms to embrace Him.'[68] And with the strange foresight of one who had long held intimate communion with his Saviour, Rutherford declared, 'This night will close the door and fasten my anchor within the veil. I shall go away in a sleep by five in the morning.' And this he did. His last recorded words were, 'Glory, glory dwelleth in Immanuel's Land', and as the shadows began to lighten on March 29th, 1661, Samuel Rutherford obeyed that summons from his superior Judge and stood at last before the King of kings.

> They've summoned me before them,
> But there I may not come, –
> My Lord says, 'Come up hither,'
> My Lord says, 'Welcome Home.'
> My kingly King, at His white throne,
> My presence doth command,
> Where glory, glory dwelleth
> In Immanuel's land.[69]

2

Marion M'Naught:
A Woman Beloved of God

'Blessed be the Lord! that in God's mercy I found in this country such a woman, to whom Jesus is dearer than her own heart.'[1] This was Samuel Rutherford's estimate of Marion M'Naught, his principal correspondent.

Few contemporary records remain to tell of the life and influence of this remarkable woman. Even her gravestone lay neglected and mouldering for many decades until it was totally lost to sight. Over two hundred years after her death it was accidentally discovered by a grave digger as he worked at a nearby grave. Blackened and broken as it was, the inscription could still be deciphered:

'Marion M'Naught, sister to John M'Naught of Kilquhanatie, an ancient and honourable baron, and spouse to William Fullerton, Provost of Kirkcudbright. Died April 1643, aged 58.'

The gravestone now appears to have vanished once more without trace, but while the *Letters of Samuel Rutherford* are read and loved by Christian people, the name of Marion M'Naught will never be forgotten.

Marion M'Naught was the daughter of the Laird of Kilquhanatie and her mother, Margaret Gordon, was the sister, or maybe half-sister, of Sir John Gordon of Lochinvar, who later became Lord Kenmure. So it was that the niece was about fifteen years older than her uncle and, living at Kirkcudbright as she did, was a frequent visitor at Kenmure Castle.

During the years when Sir John lived in careless disregard of spiritual issues the consolation and friendship of Marion M'Naught must often have revived and strengthened young Lady Jane Kenmure in the faith. In her many grievous bereavements she would find much comfort in the visits of the older woman. Following the death of Lady Jane's third little daughter, Samuel Rutherford wrote to Marion M'Naught urging her to visit the sorrowing mother: '. . . . her child is with the Lord. I entreat you, visit her . . . [for] I think she will be heavy.'[2] When Sir John himself lay dying just months later, it was his special request that his niece should come and stay at the castle and care for him together with Lady Jane until he died.

Marion M'Naught was never known by her married name. Early references uniformly use the name 'M'Naught' or sometimes 'M'Knaight', even though she had been married to William Fullerton, Provost of Kirkcudbright for many years. An acrostic is extant, written by a relative of her husband's, which extols Marion M'Naught's merits. This again is based on her maiden name. Such a practice was not unusual in those days and even today in the Scottish Highlands the custom lingers on in some areas.

Nothing is known of Marion M'Naught's childhood. She is briefly mentioned in the *Memoirs* of John Livingstone, who refers to meeting her at a communion season in Borgue in Galloway in the summer of 1626. Our first real acquaintance comes from the pages of the *Letters of Samuel Rutherford* itself. In 1627 Rutherford had begun his ministry in Anwoth. Scarcely had he and his young wife Eupham settled into the manse at Bush o'Bield close by the church when Marion M'Naught from nearby Kirkcudbright travelled across to meet the new pastor.

She and her husband William Fullerton, who held the responsible position of Provost in Kirkcudbright, had three children: a daughter, Grizzel, and two younger sons, Samuel and William. It would appear that an arrangement was made, maybe at this time, for Grizzel to come across and stay at the manse for a time, perhaps to help the young couple who had two small children. The first letter to survive from Rutherford's pen was one written to Marion M'Naught in June of that year when Rutherford was sending Grizzel back home with a trusted Christian man as escort. He expresses confidence that a work of grace had begun in the girl and promises to follow her with his prayers – a promise that he abundantly fulfilled through the years that lay ahead. So began a lifelong friendship with Marion M'Naught and her family. At least forty-seven letters found their way from Anwoth, or later Aberdeen, to Kirkcudbright – letters that must have enriched their first reader and have also brought blessing to many succeeding generations of Christians.

Marion M'Naught loved to attend the communion seasons at Anwoth. These were high days indeed in a church dedicated to the biblical traditions established by John Knox. The services, which were mainly held out-of-doors at six-monthly intervals, often extended from the Thursday or Friday of one week until the next Monday. First there were days of heart preparation and repentance before the thronging crowds drawn from all the surrounding area would join in joyful celebration of the Lord's Supper on the Sunday. A Monday preaching service of thanksgiving was established after the revival at Kirk o'Shotts in 1630, and brought the occasion to a conclusion before the people dispersed and wended their way back to their hamlets, farms and cottages. Samuel Rutherford often wrote to Marion M'Naught personally inviting her across for the occasion: 'Our Communion is on Sabbath come eight days. I will entreat you to recommend it to God, and to pray for me in that work.'[3] Perhaps it was Marion M'Naught who took down almost verbatim the words of the preacher on these occasions – words that we can still read three hundred and fifty years later and that seem almost as fresh as they did the day they were first spoken. Preaching on 'Let me hear thy voice' (*Song of Solomon 2:14*) we read, 'It is ordinary for man to beg from God, for we be but His beggars; but it is a miracle to see God beg at man. Yet here is the Potter begging from the clay; the Saviour seeking from sinners! What is His suit? It must be some great thing; it is even a sight of His bride. He is even saying to her, "My dear spouse, be kind to me, let me see thy face . . . tell me all your mind in prayer."'[4] Little wonder that Marion M'Naught loved to be there!

Alexander Whyte, speaking of the relationship that existed between Rutherford and Marion M'Naught, points out that as a good hearer delights in a good preacher, so 'where the gifts of the pulpit meet the corresponding graces in the pew you need not wonder that they recognize and delight in one another'.[5] It is evident from the correspondence that an uncommon and godly affinity of heart existed between these two. Here were kindred minds, burning with the same passion for Christ's glory and the advancement of His kingdom, and they quickly found each other out. It was to Marion M'Naught that Rutherford was able to pen some of the most moving and personal experiences of Christ's love that had been his portion in Aberdeen: 'I must tell you what lovely Jesus, fair Jesus, King Jesus hath done to my soul . . . And oh, how sweet is a fresh kiss from His holy mouth! His breathing that goeth before a kiss upon my poor soul is sweet, and hath no fault but that it is too short.'[6] To her also he discloses a glimpse into the turmoil of heart that distressed him during his early months in Aberdeen: 'My heart is sad that my days flee away, and I do no service to my Lord in His house . . . my fainting cometh before I eat, and my faith hath bowed with the sore cast, and under this almost insupportable weight! . . . Oh that it break not!'[7]

When Eupham, Rutherford's young wife, was dying it was to Marion M'Naught he confided his grief. As a helpless spectator he writes: 'My wife's disease increaseth daily, to her great torment and pain night and day . . . she sleeps none, but cries as a woman travailing in birth.'[8] Such was her distress that Rutherford could only pray that God would speedily release her from such suffering and take her to her rest. A letter written to Lady Kenmure contains no hint of his personal need but is full of concern for the spiritual welfare of his correspondent. But to Marion M'Naught he confessed, 'I have wondered why the Lord tarrieth so long. My life is bitter unto me . . . It is . . . hard to keep sight of God in a storm.'[9] It was at this time that Marion M'Naught took the practical step of sending Grizzel across to Anwoth once more to help in any way she could. After Eupham's death Grizzel cared for Rutherford when he too fell ill with a condition that kept him out of the pulpit for three months.

Not content with occasionally attending the services at Anwoth, Marion M'Naught and her husband, with others from Kirkcudbright, were behind a petition from the church there that Rutherford should leave that parish and settle in Kirkcudbright in succession to Robert Glendinning, who was now frail and elderly. Correspondence over this issue was prolonged over a period of eighteen months,[10] but although Rutherford expressed a willingness to come should it be God's will, he could get no real liberty of mind concerning the proposal. The thought of leaving his Anwoth congregation without a pastor weighed heavily on him. Thomas Sydserff, Bishop of Galloway, also intervened in the matter. Anxious to confine Rutherford's influence as much as possible, he promised the church at Kirkcudbright any man of their choosing – a rare concession indeed – if only they would not persist in their desire to call Samuel Rutherford.

These things were the cause of much searching of heart and even a degree of misunderstanding between Marion M'Naught and Samuel Rutherford. Spiritual affection for the family made the proposal very attractive but perhaps Marion M'Naught's strong desires caused her to be too pressing in the matter. 'I left you in . . . great heaviness,' Rutherford confesses, 'but I know you doubt not but that . . . my soul is knit to your soul, and to the soul of all yours . . . But by fervent calling upon my Lord, I have attained some victory over my heart . . . and over my beguiling hopes, which I know now better than I did.' However much his natural desires might dictate, he must obey his God. 'The Lord saw a nail in my heart loose, and He hath now fastened it. Honour be to His majesty.'[11]

It was inevitable that in that troubled era men and women of the stamp of Marion M'Naught and her husband should feel the stinging lash of persecution let loose upon them. Many of Rutherford's letters were written to strengthen them both in a day of trial and the theme is one recurring throughout these years: 'For Zion's sake hold not your peace, neither be discouraged, for the on-going of this persecution. Jehovah is in this burning Bush. The floods may swell and roar, but our ark shall swim above the waters; it cannot sink, because a Saviour is in it.'[12] During the early decades of the seventeenth century, crippling fines and imprisonment were often the order of the day for those who refused to compromise their Christian principles and so Rutherford writes: 'Be patient, for the Lord's sake, under the wrongs that you suffer of the wicked . . . You may not be above your Master; many a black stroke received innocent Jesus.'[13]

The Bishop of Galloway, not content with refusing permission for Samuel Rutherford to come to Kirkcudbright, had suspended the pastor, Robert Glendinning, and ordered that he should be imprisoned regardless of his age and failing health. This was because he would not accept Sydserff's choice of a successor to himself, a choice made without any regard to his earlier promises. William Fullerton, in his position of Provost of Kirkcudbright, was expected to co-operate in this matter and to incarcerate his eighty-year-old pastor. This he and the other magistrates refused to do. Instead they continued to attend Robert Glendinning's preaching and so incurred the anger of the bishop. Writing to encourage him in this stand, Rutherford says, 'Howbeit we see truth put to the worse for the time, yet Christ will be a friend to truth and will do for those who dare hazard all that they have for Him and for His glory. Sir, our fair day is coming, and the court will change, and wicked men will weep after noon, and sorer than the sons of God, who weep in the morning.'[14]

Although enabled to stand firm at this time, William Fullerton was by no means as courageous a man as Rutherford would have wished. Often he vacillated in the hour of crisis and acted below his principles. This must have brought much sorrow to Marion M'Naught, whose loyalty to Christ and His cause never wavered. Writing from Aberdeen, Rutherford says, 'Desire your husband from me, not to think ill of Christ for His cross. Many misken Christ, because He hath the cross on His back; but He will cause us all to laugh yet';[15] and again he complains, 'Your husband hath made me heavy; but be courageous in the Lord.'[16] No suffering for Christ's sake would go unrewarded, often here in this life – certainly in eternity. So Rutherford is still anxious to encourage William Fullerton and writes from his place of exile, 'I desire your husband to read this letter. I send him a prisoner's blessing. I will be obliged to him, if he will be willing to suffer for my dear Master. Suffering is the professor's golden garment; there shall be no losses on Christ's side of it.'[17]

The secret of Marion M'Naught's faith and endurance lay

not in her natural abilities and strength of character, though these were indeed present in her to a noble degree, but in the grace she derived from her constant communion with God. Above all else Marion M'Naught was a woman of prayer and this shines out again and again through the lines that Samuel Rutherford wrote to encourage and stimulate his friend in this highest of all activities. The days were difficult with the power of the Episcopal party ever on the increase and behind it, as a dark spectre, the threat of Rome itself. These things weighed heavily on the hearts of Christian people and many were prepared to suffer or even die for the principles they held dear. It was against this background that Marion M'Naught gave herself persistently and earnestly to the work of intercession.

Samuel Rutherford, however, had an unshakable faith in the ultimate triumph of the Son of God over the forces of darkness and this was a constant theme in his letters. 'Are you troubled with the case of God's kirk? . . . That broken ship will come to land, because Jesus is the pilot. Faint not; you shall see the salvation of God – else say, that God never spake His word by my mouth.'[18] Again on the same theme he writes,'To pray and believe now, when Christ seems to give you a nay-say [denial], is more than it was before. Die believing; die, and Christ's promise in your hand.'[19]

So the pastor of Anwoth encouraged his praying friend, though sometimes even he was bowed down with anxiety because of the apparent triumph of Christ's enemies. It was with Marion M'Naught that he shared his concern: 'Know that I am in great heaviness for the pitiful case of our Lord's kirk . . . I therefore entreat the aid of your prayers for myself, and the Lord's captives of hope, and for Zion.'[20] The exhortation was scarcely necessary, for Marion M'Naught gave herself to continual prayer and fasting for the revival of Christ's cause and the prosperity of the Church. Even though frail in body at times, she allowed herself no respite and

Rutherford writes to warn her in most stringent language against the folly of damaging her health. 'Remember you are in the body, and it is the lodging-house; and you may not, without offending the Lord, suffer the old walls of that house to fall down through want of necessary food . . . It is a fearful sin in us, by hurting the body by fasting, to loose one stone, or the least piece of timber in it, for the house is not your own.'[21]

Sometimes this faithful intercessor was sorely discouraged. Few seemed to share her vision, while those who did appeared to tire quickly and she received little support even from her husband. More than this, the earnest supplications she sent heavenward seemed of little avail as the situation grew darker yet. Writing from Aberdeen, Rutherford is still anxious to do all in his power to stimulate Marion M'Naught and she could hardly have received more encouraging words than these: 'Faint not, keep breath, believe; howbeit men, and husband, and friends prove weak, yet your strength faileth not . . . O woman greatly beloved! I testify and avouch it in my Lord, that the prayers ye sent to heaven these many years bygone are come up before the Lord, and shall not be forgotten . . . I charge you . . . to go on without fainting or fear, and still believe, and take no nay-say. If ye leave off, the field is lost.' He makes bold predictions of the outcome of all her praying. 'I write it (and keep this letter), utter, utter desolation shall be to your adversaries . . . The bride will yet sing, as in the days of her youth.'[22]

Marion M'Naught must have folded that letter and put it away carefully wondering whether she would ever live to see the fulfilment of Rutherford's hopes. Things were black indeed and only three weeks after this letter was written, Charles I stipulated that Archbishop Laud's new liturgy was to be read in St Giles Church, Edinburgh. But this was the historic occasion when the patience of the Scottish people broke at last, resulting in the signing of the National

Covenant amid scenes of spiritual fervour. This led in turn to a flood-tide of blessing poured out by God upon a needy people. So Marion M'Naught saw, at least in part, an answer to her supplications.

Although Samuel Rutherford, now back from his exile, rejoiced in these marvellous acts of God and was able to write, 'Our Lord has fallen to wrestle with His enemies and hath brought us out of Egypt,' yet he feared that the euphoria that gripped the people might prevent the true deep work of reformation, so urgently needed, from going forward. He writes in this same letter, 'Alas! I fear that Scotland be undone and slain with this great mercy of reformation, because there is not here that life of religion, answerable to the huge greatness of the work that dazzleth our eyes.'[23] Perhaps Rutherford's fears were well-grounded and the intermingling of political ideals with religious ardour led to some of the sad defections of future years; but there were many who rejoiced with full hearts at God's evident mercies and Marion M'Naught was surely among them.

In Marion M'Naught we find a woman of unusual astuteness of mind and with her, more than with any other correspondent, Rutherford discusses the troubling issues of church polity. He writes to her from Aberdeen begging her to go across to Anwoth to encourage his poor dispirited parishioners and counsel them to remain steadfast in the truth. She, above all others, was the mainstay of the work of Christ in Kirkcudbright. Writing from exile, he urges her to remain on in the town: 'You shall not have my advice to make haste to go out of that town; for if you remove out of Kirkcudbright, they will easily undo all. You are at God's work, and in His way there.'[24]

We can easily imagine that her death in 1643 was a sore loss to Samuel Rutherford. Six years earlier he had written these words of encouragement to his friend, 'I write it and I abide by it, God will be glorious in Marion M'Naught, when this stormy blast shall be over.'[25] The stormy blast was now over, her ship safe within the haven, and God has indeed been glorified through the life and testimony of Marion M'Naught, both in her lifetime and through succeeding generations.

3

John Gordon and his Family: My Joy and Crown

'I always saw nature mighty, lofty, heady, and strong in you; and that it was more for you to be mortified and dead to the world, than for another common man.'[1] Samuel Rutherford was under no illusions when he wrote to John Gordon of Cardoness and he had good cause for anxiety, for the Laird of Cardoness was approaching the end of life with the issues of eternity still undecided: 'Now, when ye are drinking the grounds of your cup, and ye are upon the utmost end of the last link of time, and old age, like death's long shadow, is casting a covering upon your days, it is no time to court this vain life,'[2] he wrote to try and warn the old man. John Gordon was by nature passionate and churlish and it would appear from the correspondence that he had lived a dissolute and unattractive life in former years. Even now, when subdued by age, his violent temper and unruly tongue caused much suffering to those with whom he lived.

Cardoness Castle stands on a rocky prominence at the mouth of the River Fleet about a mile from Anwoth. Its gaunt grey walls and square tower, now a tourist attraction, embody and symbolize the spirit of the stubborn old man. It was from this impregnable fortress that John Gordon intimidated his farming tenants, who grazed their cattle and eked out their meagre income from his lands.

When Samuel Rutherford first came to Anwoth, he was fearless in his denunciations of the disagreeable old laird for his unethical conduct towards his tenants. Tradition tells us that on one occasion, in a fit of passion, John Gordon drove his pastor from the castle, refusing to attend his ministry for some time. Be that as it may, an unlikely friendship sprang up between the wily old laird and his small fair-haired pastor, for behind his uncontrollable outbursts John Gordon hid a tender heart and a sensitive conscience.

That a degree of true affection existed between the Laird of Cardoness and his pastor, now exiled far away, is apparent from the tone of the four letters written from Aberdeen. Some of the most memorable descriptions of the loveliness of Christ were personally addressed to John Gordon and used as a plea to attract his affections away from earthly gain to the true source of all good. 'I dare say that angels' pens, angels' tongues, nay, as many worlds of angels as there are drops of water in all the seas, and fountains, and rivers of the earth, cannot paint Him out to you . . . Oh, what a sight to be up in heaven . . . and to see, and smell, and touch, and kiss that fair field-flower, that ever-green Tree of life! His bare shadow were enough for me.'[3]

Not only does Rutherford seek to draw his correspondent to a consideration of eternal issues by describing his Saviour in terms of winsome beauty, he is also fearless, indeed terrifying, in the stringent warnings he issues if Gordon should postpone the concerns of his soul to some more convenient season. 'Remember, when the race is ended, and the play either won or lost, and ye are in the utmost circle and border of time . . . and your poor soul shall be crying, "Lodging, lodging, for God's sake!" then shall your soul be more glad at one of your Lord's lovely and homely smiles, than if ye had the charters of three worlds for all eternity.'[4] Words such as these might seem harsh were they not mingled with moving pleas for John Gordon to act while there is still time. 'Dear Sir, my soul would mourn in secret for you, if I knew your case with God to be but false work . . . Come in, come in to Christ, and see what you want, and find it in Him,'[5] he urges.

Samuel Rutherford's dealings with John Gordon of Cardoness provide us with the finest example of his pastoral concern for those whose spiritual state seemed undecided. 'Thoughts of your soul . . . depart not from me in my sleep. Ye have a great part of my tears, sighs, supplications, and prayers. Oh, if [only] I could buy your soul's salvation with any suffering whatsoever, that ye and I might meet with joy up in the rainbow, when we shall stand before our Judge'![6] It is little wonder that his parishioners loved their pastor, for although these words were addressed to John Gordon, he extends them to include all who had been under his pastoral care. 'Sir, show the people this; for when I write to you, I think I write to you all.'[7] We are not surprised to find that the old laird of Cardoness Castle inscribed his name in a petition to the General Assembly in 1639 begging that his pastor be allowed to remain with his people in rural Anwoth and not be moved to St Andrews.

A sense of the imminence of eternity marked all Rutherford's letters in his Aberdeen days but particularly so when he corresponded with those who seemed to trifle with their eternal destiny. 'The greatest part in the world know not and will not consider that a slip in the matter of their salvation is the most pitiable slip that can be . . . Lose not the last play whatever ye do, for in that play with death your precious soul is the prize.'[8] Such thoughts led Rutherford on almost inevitably to his own yearnings for that day when he would be ushered into the divine presence and it is in this letter both to John Gordon and to the people of Anwoth that he gives expression to some of the most moving expressions of that desire: 'Oh, if He would fold the heavens together like an old cloak, and shovel time and days out of the way, and make ready in haste the

Lamb's wife for her Husband! Since He looked upon me, my heart is not mine own; He hath run away to heaven with it.'[9]

There is some evidence to suggest that old John Gordon bowed his proud head, becoming as a little child, and entered into the kingdom of heaven. 'Stoop, stoop!' Rutherford had begged, 'it is a low entry to go in at heaven's gate'[10] but in a later letter he addresses his elderly friend in this way: 'Honourable and dearest in the Lord, your letter hath refreshed my soul. My joy is fulfilled if Christ and ye be fast together. Ye are my joy and my crown.'[11] Yet even as he wrote these words, Rutherford was not entirely happy and could not forbear one further warning: 'I beseech you, by the mercies of God, and your compearance [appearing] before Christ, look Christ's accounting book and your own together, and collate them. Give the remnant of your time to your soul.'[12]

Never does Samuel Rutherford stand apart from those to whom he writes, suggesting that he himself has attained to a high degree of holiness. With disarming honesty he confesses that he too finds the path of faith and godliness perplexing at times and contrary to the natural desires of the heart. 'Believe me, that I find it to be hard wrestling to play fair with Christ, and to keep good quarters with Him,'[13] he admits, in a letter to John Gordon, and adds in a later letter, 'Heaven is not at the next door. I find Christianity to be a hard task.'[14] So it is with kindly encouragements, fearsome warnings and tender pleadings that the exiled pastor deals with John Gordon of Cardoness. We may well believe that this intractable old man was melted down under such words and found in Christ all that Rutherford had promised.

*   *   *

The path that providence had marked out for Lady Cardoness was not an easy one and the three letters that Samuel

Rutherford wrote to John Gordon's wife reveal the depth of his understanding and his concern for the individual needs of his Anwoth parishioners.

Lady Cardoness (who bore this title as a courtesy to one married to the owner of a hereditary estate) faced formidable problems in the management of the family affairs. Her husband's intemperate way of life often incurred crippling debts on the estate and Lady Cardoness, though a faithful Christian, acted as many others would have done in her circumstances: she passed on to the tenants the liability for the burden by making increased demands on them. Rutherford faced her with this injustice firmly but kindly. 'I beseech you to make conscience of your ways. Deal kindly, and with conscience, with your tenants. To fill a breach or a hole, make not a greater breach in the conscience. I wish plenty of love to your soul.'[15] Rutherford, as her pastor, not only exposed her inconsistency, but aimed to lift her thoughts and aspirations beyond material things to the eternal: 'Oh, blessed is the soul whose hope hath a face looking straight out to that day. It is not our part to make a treasure here; anything, under the covering of heaven, which we can build upon, is but ill ground and a sandy foundation.'[16]

Lady Cardoness encountered many problems in her daily life and not least the difficulty of living with a bad-tempered old man. Her husband's erratic moods and unreasonable behaviour called for a high degree of self-denial and patience. Rutherford, aware of her predicament, dealt with it in a sympathetic way: 'My counsel is, that ye bear with him when passion overtaketh him: "A soft answer putteth away wrath". Answer him in what he speaketh, and apply yourself in the fear of God to him; and then ye will remove a pound-weight of your heavy cross, that way, and so it shall become light.'[17]

In spite of some failures in Christian living, Lady Cardoness was sincere in her desire to maintain communion with

Christ in circumstances that were often unhelpful. She earnestly longed for a conscious sense of Christ's presence in her soul, yet often it seemed that He had withdrawn this awareness. Rutherford applies himself to her problem as a true pastor: 'When Christ hideth Himself, wait on, and make din till He return; it is not time then to be carelessly patient . . . Yet believe His love in a patient onwaiting and believing in the dark', and then he adds, with a touch of typical Rutherford imagery, 'Ye must learn to swim and hold up your head above the water, even when the sense of His presence is not with you to hold up your chin.'[18] He returns several times to this theme in his correspondence with Lady Cardoness and it is to her that he addresses some of his best known words on the subject: 'Learn daily both to possess and miss Christ in His secret bridegroom-smiles. He must go and come, because His infinite wisdom thinketh it best for you. We shall be together one day.'[19]

Lady Cardoness was elderly when Rutherford was corresponding with her and he uses the approaching end of her earthly pilgrimage as an incentive for godly living. Far from his mind was our present-day reluctance to refer to the subject of death in conversation with elderly Christians; rather he comes back to it again and again in the most vivid terms: 'Oh, how sweet and comfortable will the feast of a good conscience be to you, when your eye-strings shall break, your face wax pale and the breath turn cold, and your poor soul come sighing to the windows of the house of clay of your dying body, and shall long to be out . . . '[20] Such language may seem too graphic, but is no more so than many passages of Scripture dealing with the same theme. Lady Cardoness tended to place much store on earthly possessions and Rutherford sets before her the better and enduring heritage that belongs to the children of God. 'Let not the world be your portion; . . . set your heart on the inheritance'; then he urges her in meditation to make frequent 'visits' to her heavenly dwelling place. 'Go up beforehand, and see your lodging. Look through all your Father's rooms in heaven . . . be kind to the house ye are going to, and see it often.'[21]

The prayers of the banished pastor followed Lady Cardoness and her husband continually. 'Ye have a great part of my tears, sighs, supplications and prayers',[22] he writes with pathos. If there were any single human factor that kept this couple in the faith as they came to 'the utmost circle and border of time',[23] it was the intercessions of this man of God who could say: 'I beseech you by the salvation of your precious souls, and the mercies of God, to make good and sure work of your salvation.'[24]

*   *   *

If old John Gordon had sown his wild oats in his youth he certainly reaped a bitter harvest in the lives of his children and most particularly in his oldest son, John. It would appear that this young man had inherited much of his father's choleric temperament and churlish nature, finding little encouragement from his father's example to curb these natural tendencies.

Many were the occasions when Samuel Rutherford was obliged to correct the young man, but to little avail. 'I have often summoned you', wrote Rutherford, 'and now I summon you again to compear [appear] before your Judge, to make a reckoning of your life.'[25] Worse than this, John Gordon's son showed an attitude of contempt towards the public worship of God. Not daring to neglect Sunday worship altogether because of the pressure of public opinion, his sin of studied indifference was yet more dishonouring to God. Too idle to rise from his bed on time, he regularly arrived late for the service and demonstrating his lack of interest still further, added to this offence by rising from his place and leaving the building before the service was finished. Rutherford remonstrates with him for these things in a letter from Aberdeen: 'It will be a great challenge to you before God . . . if ye turn aside after the fashions of this world, and if ye go not in time to the kirk, to wait on the public worship of God, and if ye tarry not at it, till all the exercises of religion be ended.'[26]

The younger John Gordon filled up his cup of wrath during the week: drinking into the night and womanizing, though he was a married man, were but two of the vices that characterized him. 'Forsake the follies of deceiving and vain youth . . . ,' Rutherford begs, 'whoring, night-drinking, and the misspending of the Sabbath.'[27] Yet all this catalogue of ungodliness paled in Rutherford's mind before Gordon's one great sin of spurning God's gracious offer of salvation through Christ, for this he says 'will burn up your soul with the terrors of the Almighty, when your awakened conscience shall flee in your face.'[28]

Many another pastor might have despaired of so profligate a young man, but Samuel Rutherford looked beyond the apparent indifference to the feeble attempts at reformation he had observed and tried to encourage young John Gordon in his endeavour: 'Be not discouraged at broken and spilled resolutions,' he urges and then adds, 'but to it, and to it again!'[29] He uses every weapon in his armoury to destroy Gordon's unbelief: he warns, threatens, pleads and again and again points to that day 'when ye are upon the border of eternity, and your one foot out of time'. Repentance will then be too late and 'Oh then, ten thousand thousand floods of tears cannot extinguish these flames, or purchase to you one hour's release from that pain.'[30]

Two letters were written to John Gordon's erring son from Rutherford's period in exile. It would seem that they appear in the wrong order in Bonar's edition of *Rutherford's Letters*, for in Letter 123 Rutherford refers to a letter written earlier and thanks Gordon for a reply he has received. This is probably Letter 173. By the time he wrote the second letter, young John Gordon had clearly thought deeply on eternal issues and this letter is gentler in tone. Not only had Gordon received a stern rebuke from his pastor but God had also been dealing with him through the death of some of his children. Possibly an epidemic had swept through the castle, with its dank thick walls and chill rooms, removing three or four little ones from the family circle. Young Gordon and his wife were heart-broken but the loss that hurt most was that of little Barbara – maybe the oldest child. Rutherford had a special and unusual word of consolation for the grieving parents concerning this child: 'For your bairns, now at rest (I speak to you and your wife, and cause her to read this), I am a witness for Barbara's glory in heaven.'[32] It is difficult to know exactly what Rutherford means by this: at the least he is assured of the spiritual security of the child. But from the context it would appear that he means more than this, for he distinguishes Barbara from the other little ones who had so recently died. Of these he speaks generally, 'They are not lost to you that are laid up in Christ's treasury in heaven,' but of Barbara he speaks specifically, maintaining that he can testify of a certainty that she is in glory. Perhaps as the banished pastor pored over the letter bringing the distressing news, God granted a particular inward assurance of faith amounting almost to sight that it was 'well with the child' and that Barbara was indeed in glory. It would be wrong to go further than this in an interpretation of these words. However it is at this point that Alexander Whyte takes an extraordinary flight of fancy and embroiders the narrative in this way: 'One day when Rutherford was in the Spirit in his silent prison, whether in the body or out of the body, he was caught up into Paradise to see the beauty of his Lord, and to hear his little daughter singing Glory. And among the thousands of children that sang round the throne he told young Cardoness that he saw and heard little Barbara Gordon, whose death had broken every heart in Cardoness Castle. 'I give you my word for it,' wrote Rutherford to her broken-hearted father, 'I saw two Anwoth children there, and one of them was your child and one of them was mine.'[32] Though beautiful, this is unwarranted speculation and could lead many to discredit Rutherford's words here and therefore in other respects.[33]

Although subdued by grief, Gordon's soul was still unconverted and in Letter 123 Rutherford plies him with thirteen unanswerable arguments why he should attend urgently to matters of eternity. Some he had used before but he repeats them unashamedly: 'Think what ye would give for an hour when ye shall lie like dead, cold, blackened clay';[34] but many arguments are new and designed to woo John Gordon into the way of God. 'Consider what joy and peace are in Christ's service . . . What dignity it is to be a son of God.'[35]

So the Gordon family pass from the annals of recorded history and only eternity will reveal 'the secret things that belong unto the Lord our God'.[36] However, there is one further mention of the younger John Gordon that suggests that he did indeed reform his ways by the grace of God and become his pastor's joy and crown at the last day. This is in a letter of his preserved among the Wodrow manuscripts written while he was fighting with the Covenanter army in the Civil War. Dated March 1644 and written from Sunderland, it breathes a very different spirit from that of the arrogant young man of former days. Rutherford had earlier had to urge Gordon to deal tenderly with his wife and in no way to abuse her; now Gordon writes to Thomas Wylie, 'I entreat you to be kind to my wife . . . Be earnest with her that she seek a nearer acquaintance with Christ: and fail not to pray for her and her family, and me.'[37]

'I long to hear whether or not your soul be hand-fasted

with Christ,'[38] Rutherford had written seven years earlier, and we may assume from these words that, in the life of the younger John Gordon of Cardoness at least, God granted him his heart's desire.

4

John Stuart and John Kennedy: Faithful in Life and Death

On the west coast of Scotland stands the town of Ayr. It has long held an honoured place in the annals of Christianity for its indissoluble connection with the ministry of John Welsh between the years 1600 and 1605. Born not long before the death of John Knox, Welsh not only became Knox's son-in-law by his marriage to Elizabeth Knox, but in his life also he bore a noble tribute to the beauty and power of true Christianity restored under the great reformer's leadership. Prodigal in his youth, even to the extent of joining a roving band of robbers, Welsh was powerfully converted to God and devoted his life to the work of preaching. He became known as a man of prayer and considered it a wasted day if he had not been able to give many hours to this exercise. Even in the night the burden of the souls of men lay so heavily upon him that he regularly rose to pray while others slept. When he first went to Ayr from Kirkcudbright, the town was notorious for its wickedness. No-one would so much as offer the new minister any accommodation until a merchant by the name of John Stuart kindly gave him a 'prophet's chamber' in his home. In those early days of his short ministry in Ayr, John Welsh was often obliged to intervene physically in the angry street brawls. Gradually, however, by his example, by the power of his prayers and by the tender constraints of his preaching which few could hear without tears, God wrought an astonishing change throughout the town.

John Stuart's hospitality was abundantly rewarded. We can believe that this young merchant, later to become Provost of Ayr, profited much from the presence of such a man under his roof. Although suffering all his life from a serious speech impediment so that it was hard for others to understand him at times, John Stuart would regularly join his pastor in times of prayer and fellowship together with another friend, Hugh Kennedy. We are told by John Livingstone that whenever Stuart prayed in public, he seemed to be given relief from his handicap and attained a remarkable clarity of speech. As time went on, others joined this small gathering and these occasions became a great stimulus to Christian living. Great was the loss to the town of Ayr when John Welsh was served with a prison sentence and then banishment fifteen months later in 1606, in retaliation for his presence at a General Assembly of the Church convened against the dictates of the power-seeking monarch, James VI.

Much about Stuart's friend, Hugh Kennedy, has been forgotten, but two notable facts have survived the passing centuries. The first was the way he prayed. Doubtless under the example of a man like John Welsh, Hugh Kennedy aspired to a degree of communion with God unusual even in those unusual days. He has been described as 'a mighty wrestler with God' and we learn that when the plague was raging in Ayr, leaving its havoc of bereavement and disaster, Hugh Kennedy gave himself to earnest intercession until the course of the disease was halted. It is no surprise that Welsh, exiled in France, could write: 'Happy is that city, yea, happy is that nation that has a Hugh Kennedy in it.'[1] The second astonishing fact about this man was the way he died. Robert Wodrow tells us in his life of *Robert Boyd of Trochrig* that on his death-bed Hugh Kennedy was 'filled with inexpressible joy in the Holy Ghost, beyond what it is possible to comprehend'.

After his friend's death, Stuart extended to Kennedy's son, John, that warmth of friendship he had shown his father. He would have encouraged the younger man in the same godly ways, and from the testimony of those who knew John Kennedy it would seem that he was indeed a worthy son of such a man. Robert Fleming in his *Fulfilling of the Scriptures* comments that John Kennedy was as choice a Christian as any he knew.

A less direct but perhaps more revealing tribute is found in the three letters written to John Kennedy by Samuel Rutherford. Ayr lies little more than fifty miles from Anwoth and it is likely that John Stuart and John Kennedy travelled across from time to time to benefit from the ministry there. Perhaps they attended the communion seasons, we do not know, but it is certain that Rutherford knew both these men personally. Exiled far north to Aberdeen, Rutherford longed for the encouragement of letters from his friends, and it is to John Kennedy that the imprisoned pastor commits one of the most exalted descriptions of the love of Christ to be found anywhere in his three hundred and sixty-five letters: ' . . . I cannot think, but that, at the first sight I shall see of that most lovely and fairest face, love will come out of his two eyes, and fill me with astonishment . . . O Well-beloved, run, run fast! . . . O fair day, when wilt thou dawn! O shadows, flee away! I think hope and love, woven through other, make our absence from Christ spiritual torment.'[2] Such words as these leave us strangely out of our depth but clearly Rutherford felt happy to entrust them to John Kennedy. We can well assume that John was a man of prayer like his father before him, for it is to him that Rutherford complains of the shallow professions of many who claimed Christianity and exclaims: 'But a bed watered with tears, a throat dry with praying, eyes as a fountain of tears for the sins of the land, are rare to be found among us. Oh if we could know the power of godliness!'[3]

To Rutherford's Anwoth days belongs one incident of

interest involving both John Stuart and John Kennedy. When John Stuart had inherited a little money, his first thought had been to share it among some of Christ's servants passing through difficult days. This he did, but not long afterwards he himself ran into financial problems and was obliged to leave the country to trade overseas for a short time. Prospered in his purpose, he was soon able to load a ship with all his merchandise and then return himself to Ayr by a quicker route to await the arrival of his vessel.

Long weeks passed without any news of the ship until at last rumours reached Ayr that it had been captured by the Turks. Deep gloom settled on the hearts of the friends of this generous merchant. But one day his missing vessel appeared on the horizon and jubilation spread through the town at the news. John Kennedy in his enthusiasm leapt into a small boat and set off to greet the ship. Scarcely had he done so when a boisterous wind whipped the waves to a fury. Soon his little craft was driven helplessly along and then to the dismay of all on shore it disappeared from view. John Kennedy must surely be drowned!

John Stuart was heartbroken. The loss of his friend was a calamity far greater than that of his vessel. Stunned with grief, he shut himself up in his room for three days, allowing none to interrupt the melancholy of his thoughts. At last he emerged from his seclusion and made his way to Kennedy's home to solace the widow. It is not difficult to imagine his astonishment when John Kennedy himself suddenly walked in at the door. His boat had been driven from sight beyond the larger ship and then grounded on a distant part of the coast.

Samuel Rutherford was not slow to make use of these providential circumstances for Kennedy's spiritual profit and wrote urging him to be prepared for death whenever it should strike. John Kennedy had witnessed the amazing scenes that accompanied his father's death, but Rutherford knew that it takes more than example to prepare a man to die well. So he writes, 'Death hath not bidden you farewell, but hath only left you for a short season. End your journey ere the night come upon you. Have all in readiness against the time that ye must sail through that black and impetuous Jordan . . . ye can die but once, and if ye mar or spill that business, ye cannot come back to mend that piece of work again.'[4] He ends this letter with one more reminder of John's father and his prayerful life: 'Good brother, call to mind the memory of your worthy father, now asleep in Christ; and, as his custom was, pray continually, and wrestle for the life of a dying, breathless kirk.'[5] He concludes with a message for John Stuart: 'Remember my dearest love to John Stuart, whom I love in Christ . . . I do always remember him and hope for a meeting. The Lord Jesus establish him more and more, though he be already a strong man in Christ.'[6] Stuart meanwhile had been able to sell all his commodities, clear his debts and still live comfortably on what remained.

Throughout this period Charles 1 (who had succeeded his father to the throne in 1625), strove to gain total supremacy in the Scottish Church and to increase his stranglehold by means of his bishops. By 1637 Archbishop Laud's new liturgy was shortly to become compulsory and each minister ordered to obtain two copies. Many good men felt they could no longer tolerate this erosion of all they held dear and preferred to leave the security of home and emigrate to a place where they could worship without compromise of conscience.

So it was that John Stuart, now probably turned sixty years of age, joined with John Livingstone, Robert Blair and many others in an attempt to emigrate to New England. For many months and with continual set-backs, they built their ship called *Eagle Wing*. At last, six months behind schedule, it was ready and over one hundred and forty people went on board. But the voyage seemed doomed to failure and after only a few weeks at sea the severe weather conditions forced a speedy return home.

It was against this background of bewilderment and disappointment that Samuel Rutherford wrote a letter to John Stuart that must be amongst the finest of all he wrote: 'Kiss His wise and unerring providence . . . Learn to believe Christ better than His strokes, Himself and His promises better than His glooms . . . Let not the Lord's dealings seem harsh, rough, or unfatherly, because it is unpleasant. When the Lord's blessed will bloweth across your desires, it is best, in humility, to strike sail to Him, and to be willing to be led any way our Lord pleaseth.'

Strong belief in the providence of God overruling all circumstances for His people shines out again and again in Rutherford's correspondence with John Stuart: 'Let God make of you what He will, He will end all with consolation, and will make glory out of your sufferings.'[7] Little did he know that within eighteen months of the return of *Eagle Wing*, God would intervene on behalf of His people. With the signing of the National Covenant, the strength of the Episcopal party was to be so impaired that many of these men (but most notably Blair and Livingstone) were able to enjoy long and unmolested ministries.

Not long after these events, John Stuart's pilgrim days were over. He found dying hard. Unlike his friend Hugh Kennedy, Stuart knew little joy on his death bed. All assurance of his acceptance in Christ seemed to melt away in his time of need. 'I doubt myself,' he cried out in his extremity, 'and am in great agony, yea, at the brink of despair.' It could well be that in his need he read over and over again some words recently written to him by Samuel Rutherford: 'The stability of our heaven is in God . . . Oh sweet stability of sure bottomed salvation! Who could win heaven, if this were not so? . . . Oh, God be thanked that our salvation is coasted, and landed, and shored upon Christ, who is Master of winds and storms!'[8] Just two days before he died, the storm was stilled for John Stuart and he was able to declare: 'I have been fighting and working out my salvation with fear and trembling, and now I bless God it is perfect, sealed, confirmed, and all fears are gone.'[9]

5

David Dickson:
He Showed Me All My Heart

'From Irvine, being on my journey to Christ's Palace in Aberdeen, August 4th 1636.' So runs the inscription on a letter written by Samuel Rutherford to Robert Cunningham, another servant of Christ called upon to suffer for the sake of the truth. The ecclesiastical court that had met in Edinburgh in July of that year had passed an order of banishment on Rutherford, stipulating that he should report in Aberdeen by August 20. So with some days to spare, he had first journeyed west to Irvine to spend time with his friend, David Dickson.

Since entering the ministry in 1618, David Dickson had preached at Irvine with the exception of a short period when he too had been banished to the north of Scotland for his refusal to compromise his principles over the Articles of Perth, ratified by law in 1621 and intended to re-introduce pre-Reformation forms into church worship. Here was a kindred spirit indeed and we can only guess at the warmth of fellowship those two men shared in the time allowed to them. Doubtless Dickson, who was seventeen years the senior, would have encouraged Rutherford with his own testimony of God's goodness in time of trial and assured him that Christ would sweeten his sufferings with comforts of grace. Perhaps he told his friend of that day when God came to him and filled his soul with 'such joy and approbation . . . that he scarcely ever had the like in all his life.'[1] This was God's answer of approval when Dickson had steadfastly withstood the pressure brought upon him even by Christian friends to swerve from his fearless stand over the Articles of Perth for which he had been exiled. Maybe they talked together of the glorious end of sorrow for the children of God and urged each other on in the sure anticipation of the ultimate triumph of the cause of Christ.

The letter that Rutherford wrote from Irvine takes pride of place as Letter 1 in M'Ward's first edition of *Mr Rutherford's Letters*, setting the tone for the whole. It retains this position in most subsequent editions, including one as late as 1875, edited by Dr Thomas Smith. Its themes may well reflect the topics covered by Dickson and Rutherford as they spoke together. Certainly Rutherford was sometimes cast down as he faced the prospect of banishment: 'I am a faint, dead-hearted, cowardly man, oft borne down, and hungry in waiting for the marriage supper of the Lamb.' But the hope of glory sustained his spirit: 'When I look over beyond the line, and beyond death, to the laughing side of the world, I triumph, and ride upon the high places of Jacob.'[2]

Rutherford and Dickson were men of like mind. Dickson, born in 1583, was also an excellent scholar, preacher and pastor. Both had a poetic strain in their natures and Dickson had written several well-loved poems. 'O mother dear, Jerusalem' was the title of one of his best known. John Livingstone in his *Memoirs* includes delightful pen sketches of 'ministers in the Church of Scotland eminent for grace and gifts, for faithfulness and success'[3] and as David Dickson was a close friend of Livingstone's, he recounts interesting details of Dickson's life.

Livingstone tells us that Dickson 'was a man singularly gifted with an edifying way of preaching',[4] and able to follow up such preaching with a penetrating understanding of the human heart. Men and women in spiritual need and perplexity would travel from many miles around to seek counsel from the pastor of Irvine. Little wonder then that the

English merchant who heard Rutherford and Blair preach at St Andrews about the year 1650 also comments that in Irvine he heard 'a well-favoured proper old man with a long beard and that man showed me all my heart.'[5]

A brazen act of literary piracy has secured for posterity a choice little account of the life and ministry of David Dickson. A man by the name of George Sinclair translated a Latin treatise of Dickson's and published it under the title *Truth's Victory over Error*, with his own name affixed. Any kudos was short-lived because Robert Wodrow, whose own fame rests on his monumental work, *The History of the Sufferings of the Church of Scotland* published in 1722, promptly republished the treatise in 1684 with its rightful author's name and added a biographical sketch.

This sketch supplements much of our information about Dickson's ministry at Irvine. His early years there had proved to be an era of God's manifest power as revivals spread through all the west of Scotland. Stewarton, only eight miles from Irvine, witnessed moving scenes as God displayed His grace and many were convicted and converted. David Dickson would often travel across and with sensitivity and wisdom counsel the people, dealing tenderly with wounded consciences. Scarcely a week passed during these days but that some were effectively converted through the power of God.

From Wodrow's sketch we learn interesting details of Dickson's style of preaching – details that John Howie later incorporated into his chapter on Dickson in *The Scots Worthies*, first published in 1775. 'I have some of Mr Dickson's sermons at Irvine, taken from his mouth. They are full of solid substantial matter, very spiritual, and in a very familiar style, not low, but extremely strong, plain and effecting. It is somewhat akin to Mr Rutherford's in his admirable *Letters*.'[6] We are not surprised then that Rutherford and Dickson should have had so much in common.

David Dickson is chiefly remembered today by his writings. A plan had been inaugurated amongst several ministers of that day to write short commentaries on many of the books of the Bible, aiming above all to help ordinary Christians to love and understand the Word of God. From a reference in one of Rutherford's letters it is clear that Dickson's work on the *Epistle to the Hebrews*, published in 1635, was already in demand.[7] His later contributions on the other epistles and on *Matthew's Gospel* and the *Psalms* were also popular. These works are still read and valued even today, though more than three hundred years have elapsed since they were first published.[8]

Rutherford planned to write a commentary on Hosea, but this he never achieved. His main contribution to the scheme, however, was a commentary on Isaiah. He gave himself to this work with unrelenting diligence during the last years of life, fearful lest he should die leaving the task unfinished. It was to be his literary 'magnum opus' and Robert M'Ward tells us 'his heart travailed more in the birth of this piece than ever I knew him of any.' He was willing to have 'his heaven suspended for a season',[9] M'Ward adds, if only he might finish the work. This was the manuscript that was lost when many of Rutherford's papers were confiscated and taken to London at the Restoration.

*   *   *

So it was that, after a few days with David Dickson, Rutherford continued on his way to Aberdeen. Four letters found their way to the manse at Irvine from his period of lonely exile. Heart speaks to heart and these letters demonstrate the depths of friendship and trust that the two men shared. Rutherford is able to confide his sorrows: 'I am often laid in the dust with challenges and apprehensions of His anger and then, if a mountain of iron were laid upon me, I cannot be heavier.' But sweeter far were the revelations of Christ's love that he was favoured to experience: 'My life is joy; and such joy through His comforts, as I have been afraid lest I should shame myself and cry out, for I can scarce bear what I get. Had I known what He was keeping for me, I should never have been so faint-hearted.'[10]

It was wrong to seek to live on experiences and Rutherford acknowledges this to Dickson: 'I would fain learn not to idolize comfort, sense, joy, and sweet felt presence . . . the Bridegroom Himself is better than all the ornaments that are about Him.'[11] And it is also to Dickson that Rutherford confides that some of his highest experiences of Christ's conscious presence were only fleeting in nature: 'Sometimes, while I have Christ in my arms, I fall asleep in the sweetness of His presence, and He, in my sleep, stealeth away out of my arms; and when I awake, I miss Him.'[12]

Sorrows overwhelmed Rutherford at times. Wistfully he thought of the joys of worship in Anwoth and could even envy the 'sparrows and swallows that build their nests in the Kirk of Anwoth, blessed birds.'[13] But he turns his sad thoughts to good purpose in a stimulating letter to David Dickson: 'I pray God that ye never have the woeful and dreary experience of a closed mouth; for then ye shall judge the sparrows that may sing on the church of Irvine, blessed birds. O man of God, go on, go on . . . I dare write, that Christ will be glorified in David Dickson, howbeit Scotland be not gathered.'[14]

Without doubt God had further purposes for Dickson, for he played a strategic role in the events leading up to the historic signing of the National Covenant. During the remainder of that unforgettable year Dickson's wisdom and learning were used under God's hand and most particularly at the crucial General Assembly that was held in Glasgow in November 1638. In August 1639 he was chosen almost unanimously as the Moderator of the next General Assembly to be held in Edinburgh, so demonstrating the esteem in which he was held. In 1648 there came from his pen a work entitled *Therapeutica Sacra* or *Cases of Conscience Resolved*. In this way he passed on to posterity the gathered fruits of his years of pastoral counselling. This book was considered by his contemporaries to be his most important. Happily, the same wisdom and understanding of the human heart shines through in his commentaries and so is not lost to us today.

In David Dickson's family circumstances he experienced much trial, as a number of his children died in the early years of life. A last letter from Rutherford to Dickson, written in 1640, has survived the centuries and is an example of the great letter-writer's ability to console the bereaved. One secret of his effectiveness lay in a sensitivity of spirit that felt the griefs of others as if they had been his own. On hearing of his friend's bereavement, Rutherford is said to have called for pen and ink declaring: 'When one arm is broken off and bleeds, it makes the other bleed with it.'[15] Only a meek acquiescence in the sovereign will of God can calm the heart, Rutherford maintained in this letter to David Dickson. This sorrow was 'lustred with mercy', he assures his friend, and his affection shines out clearly in the final exhortation: 'Dearest brother, go on, and faint not. Something of yours is in heaven, beside the flesh of your exalted Saviour; and ye go on after your own.'[16]

'I am made of extremes',[17] Rutherford once confessed to Dickson and this was demonstrated most painfully in the experience of these two men during the 1650s. As already noted, they were found on opposing sides of the controversy between the Resolutioners and the Protesters that rent the Scottish Church throughout that decade. Dickson, who was by then Professor of Divinity at Edinburgh University, espoused the Resolutionist position and his influence can be traced behind many of the pamphlets that poured off the presses urging its case. Rutherford, on the other hand, supported the Protesters' cause but he was sadly guilty of bitter invective in propagating his views. Dr A.B. Grosart speaks of Rutherford's attitudes in grieved astonishment, maintaining that they demonstrate 'such assumption of personal infallibility . . . such unmeasured vituperation . . . and such suspicion of all who differed from him as is alike wonderful and sorrowful.'[18]

It would seem that the Resolutioners' views were coloured by the critical need for the unity of the nation in an hour of crisis. However, without any doubt the Protesters stood firm on the principles that lay at the heart of the National Covenant, and even Dickson is said to have admitted this on his death-bed in 1662. 'I must confess, madam,' he said to a lady who came to visit him, 'that the Protesters have been much truer prophets than we were.'[19]

Samuel Rutherford, though many years younger, ended his pilgrimage before his friend. After a long and useful life, David Dickson was also to experience something of the malicious treachery of Charles 11, who dismissed him from his position as Professor of Divinity in Edinburgh. But Dickson had his eyes set on an eternal kingdom and was able to say to John Livingstone, a fellow-sufferer for Christ's sake, just days before he died: 'I have taken all my good deeds and all my bad deeds and cast them through each other in a heap before the Lord, and have betaken me to Jesus Christ and in Him I have full and sweet peace.'[20]

6

Robert Blair:
A Sweet Majestic-Looking Man

'Suffering is the other half of our ministry, howbeit the hardest,'[1] Samuel Rutherford wrote to Robert Blair as he began the seventh month of his exile from Anwoth and the enforced silence from his dearest joy: the preaching of the gospel of Christ. Robert Blair was a fellow-sufferer in that same cause. Born in Irvine in 1593, he exercised his ministry throughout the same period as Rutherford and often these men had cause to strengthen and encourage each other to stand fast in an evil day.

Unlike Rutherford, Robert Blair came under powerful influences of the Spirit of God very early in life. While Rutherford grieved over a wasted youth, young Blair was serious in his religious concern throughout childhood. His father, who was 'addicted to prayer',[2] as Blair himself tells us, died when the child was but five years of age, leaving a family of six children behind, with Robert the youngest. Robert's mother, who lived a widow for fifty years, was unconverted at the time and remained so throughout Robert's childhood. Not until David Dickson began his ministry at Irvine in 1618 was she at last brought into the kingdom of God.

Robert first felt a concern for his own spiritual state when as a child of seven he heard a sermon he could never forget. It was from the lips of an English preacher ejected from his ministry by the pressure of the bishops. Writing of this sermon sixty-three years later, Blair could say, 'The countenance, carriage and voice of the speaker remain fresh upon my memory.'[3] When he himself entered the ministry, he preached on the same text that he had heard that day.[4]

At the age of eleven, Robert was seriously ill with what would appear to be a form of tuberculosis – the same condition that had carried his father to the grave. This time of illness was used by God to bring the child to an assurance of faith and soon he expressed a desire to be admitted to the Lord's Table.

When he was sixteen years of age, Blair furthered his studies by attending the College of Glasgow, as the university was then called, concentrating particularly on the study of philosophy. It was here that a life-long friendship was forged with David Dickson, who had lectured in philosophy at Glasgow for eight years prior to his preaching ministry in Irvine. The two men had much in common and Blair could write that they enjoyed 'a most entire friendship and a covenant of mutual remembrance one of another frequently before the Lord'.[5]

Shortly before Blair himself began preaching in 1622, he was favoured with an unusual visitation of the Spirit of God to his soul. It was during another period of severe illness and though his body had been burning with fever and wracked with pain so that he felt himself to be a dying man, he tells us, 'The love of God, burning more fervently in my soul, made me feel no pain at all.' Anticipating the glory awaiting him, he was able to sing with fervour the last words of Psalm 16: 'In thy presence is fulness of joy; at thy right hand there are pleasures for evermore.'[6]

In these ways God prepared His servant for a ministry of exceptional usefulness in Bangor, Northern Ireland, where he went in 1623. News of his preaching soon spread far and wide and we read of people flocking in from country areas to hear him. Many were powerfully converted, for these were days of God's right hand both in Ireland and in Scotland. It is not surprising that the Evil One was soon active to stir up opposition to Robert Blair's ministry and in 1632 the Bishop of Down suspended him from preaching on some trumped-up accusation. Although this was later withdrawn, the damage was done and Blair was obliged to travel to London to sort out the situation at Court and renew his permission to preach.

It was these circumstances that led to the first known meeting between Blair and Rutherford. On his way back to Ireland, Blair determined to visit Galloway and meet the pastor of Anwoth, whose Christ-exalting preaching had become a by-word in the land. Time, however, was at a premium, for while Blair was in London, a vivid dream and a Scripture reading that seemed to corroborate the dream convinced him that his wife, Beatrix, was either dying or had died. The long journey home on horseback with its hours of vain speculation only added to his distress.

As he approached Galloway, Blair felt a desire also to meet Marion M'Naught but knew he could not spare time for both visits. Torn by indecision, he prayed for direction from God and then, throwing the horse's rein across its neck, allowed the animal to choose its own path. Given free rein, the horse found the road to Kirkcudbright more congenial and soon Blair was knocking at the home of Marion M'Naught and her husband. To his delight he found Rutherford himself there as well, visiting his friend and correspondent. Blair's desires were abundantly fulfilled and he reported that he was 'greatly refreshed with their company'.[7]

With heavy heart Blair covered the last homeward miles, dreading what he might find on his return. It appears, however, that before arriving he gained some assurance that this dream was a warning of future events, and so it proved. Just sixteen months later, Beatrix, who had often enjoyed a close walk and communion with God, ended her earthly pilgrimage, leaving Robert with the care of their three small children. This bereavement Blair found grievous indeed: the uncommon sweetness of Beatrix' disposition, her prayers and companionship were a loss heavy to be borne and his spirit nearly broke under the sorrow.

Although the trip to London had been successful, the opposition to Blair's ministry continued, ending finally with threats and excommunication. So now with little to detain him, Blair decided to emigrate to New England where he might preach freely and perhaps find healing for his grieving spirit.

It was in 1636 that he joined with John Livingstone, John Stuart and about one hundred and forty others in an attempt to make the voyage. But as we have seen, this venture was beset with problems. After only a few weeks of good progress weather conditions became so hazardous that their ship, *Eagle Wing*, was obliged to turn homeward once more.

Samuel Rutherford, exiled in Aberdeen, followed these events with interest. Writing from Irvine 'on my journey to Christ's Palace in Aberdeen', he expressed his concern: 'I know not . . . if our worthy brethren be gone to sea or not. They are on my heart and in my prayers.'[8] When he heard all that had transpired he was quick to write to John Stuart, John Livingstone and Robert Blair, knowing well how puzzled and dispirited his friends would be. As a true pastor he was anxious to forestall the criticism that many might voice in suggesting that events proved that these Christians had mistaken the will of God. He illustrates from Scripture that difficulties in themselves are no certain indication that a course of action is contrary to God's will: indeed, many examples could be given to show that the purposes of God must often be accomplished through apparently insurmountable problems. The willingness of his friends to risk life and health in order to serve God in accordance with conscience was a demonstration of a heart of love for the truth. Suffering must ever be the portion of Christ's believing people. 'It is folly to think to steal to heaven with a whole skin,' Rutherford reminds Blair, but as one sufferer to another he adds with triumph, 'Dear brother, upon my salvation, this is His truth that we suffer for . . . Courage, courage! . . . joy, joy for evermore!'[9]

Robert Blair had remarried before the voyage of *Eagle Wing* and throughout that tempestuous journey his young wife, Catherine, struggled to nurse an infant son. It was an inauspicious beginning to life and little William was clearly unable to gain strength. Yet the Lord heard the mother's prayer that her son should not die at sea and it was not until after she and Robert had returned to Belfast that the child died. The second Mrs Blair followed in the noble tradition of many godly women of that generation who counted all things loss for Christ's sake.

Blair continued to preach in spite of opposition but when a plot for his capture was discovered, he escaped with his family back to his home town of Irvine. Here trouble still followed him and he was prohibited from preaching. Once again he attempted to leave the country, this time as chaplain to a regiment stationed in France, but was frustrated in his design. Gradually the purpose behind these mysterious providences began to unfold and through the determination of his first wife's sister, Barbara Hamilton, and other stalwart women, who presented a petition on his behalf to the Privy Council, Blair was granted permission to preach freely once more. By 1638, shortly after the signing of the National Covenant, Blair accepted an invitation to the preaching ministry at Ayr.

The people of Ayr, having suffered under the ministry of a hireling who had fled soon after the signing of the Covenant, loved their new pastor. It was with much sorrow that pastor and people heard only months later that the General Assembly wished Blair to move to St Andrews to fill a position left vacant by one of the episcopal ministers removed by the terms of the Covenant. His people's pleas availed a little and gained a year's reprieve, but by 1639 the Assembly would brook no more delay and Blair had no alternative but to go. Providentially, by the same Assembly Rutherford was also requested to move to St Andrews to become Professor of Divinity at St Mary's College. Rutherford, too, was distressed by the request. But he, too, had to yield and turn his face away from Anwoth for the last time, but not before he had gained the concession that he should become Robert Blair's colleague in the ministry in addition to his academic work.

So began twenty years of partnership, interrupted only by the four years Rutherford spent in London working on the Westminster Confession of Faith. Both Rutherford and Blair were men of outstanding, though differing, gifts. The evaluation by an English merchant visiting St Andrews has often been quoted: 'I went to St Andrews,' he says, 'where I heard a sweet majestic-looking man (Blair) and he showed me the majesty of God. After him I heard a little fair man (Rutherford) and he showed me the loveliness of Christ.'[10] Under the influence of two such men, many students were trained for the ministry and learnt principles of godliness which enabled them to endure the baptism of fire so soon to overtake the Covenanting Church of Jesus Christ. Donald Cargill was only one of many whose life and testimony bore clear evidence of such influence. In his martyr-death over thirty years later, he suffered for those same strong principles he had learnt from the lips of Rutherford during his student days at St Andrews.

The ten years following the coronation of Charles II at Scone in 1651 make sad reading for lovers of Scottish church history, for these were days when the Church was torn to shreds by the controversy of the Resolutioners and the Protesters. Oliver Cromwell, looking in astonished dismay at the spectacle of rival General Assemblies, each condemning the other, forbade any further Assemblies of the Church during his Protectorate.

Robert Blair, ever a peace-loving man, was much distressed by the controversy, particularly at seeing his two friends Samuel Rutherford and David Dickson on opposing sides, and he did all in his power to reconcile the factions. He was especially grieved when the presses began to pour forth leaflets for and against the Public Resolutions which had sparked off the dispute. These were often accompanied by ungodly invective and he called them 'our weakness-discovering writings, and papers that do not heal but augment our divisions and cast more oil in the flame'.[11] The path of the peace-maker is hard and often incurs the misunderstanding of both parties and this was Blair's sad experience. He received little thanks for his pains during his lifetime.

As we have seen, David Dickson and also many others came to recognize the flaws of the Resolutioners' position which they had so heatedly defended when the hidden malice and deceitfulness of Charles II became manifest at the Restoration. But the damage was done: the Drunken Parliament of 1661, made up of many enemies of the Covenants, did all in its power to reverse the recent progress of the Reformation and set the scene for the long years of persecution that were to come.

By the beginning of 1661, it was clear that Samuel Rutherford was dying. Robert Blair who was frequently at his friend's bedside during that last illness was favoured to hear some of the memorable words that he spoke. Gone were the controversies of recent days, as the light of eternity shone more brightly. 'Mine eyes shall see my Redeemer,' Rutherford murmured to Blair, 'and what would you have more? There is an end,' and again, 'there is an end.' And in the light of that end he was able to say, 'I have been a single [minded] man, but I stand at the best pass that ever a man did. Christ is mine and I am His.'[12] In the last hours of Rutherford's life, Blair heard words that have been the priceless heritage of the Christian Church ever since. 'What think ye now of Christ?' Blair had asked. 'I shall live and adore Him', responded the dying man. 'Glory, glory to my Creator and Redeemer for ever! Glory shines in Immanuel's land.'[13]

This brought to a close a partnership of kindred hearts that had guided and moulded the Scottish Church through all the vicissitudes of the period known as the Second Reformation. Rutherford was spared the knowledge of the cruel martyr deaths of his friends James Guthrie, Lord Warriston and the Marquis of Argyll, but Blair's earthly course had five years yet to run and sad years they were. Ousted from St Andrews by the intrigues of the 'Judas of the Scottish Church', Archbishop James Sharp, Blair retired to Kirkcaldy. Even that did not satisfy the Archbishop, who feared Blair's influence, so at last Blair settled in a small village near Aberdour. He had not been there for long, before, worn with sorrow, he joined Rutherford once more, but now in 'Immanuel's high and blessed land'.[14]

7

Lady Boyd:
A Rare Pattern of Christianity

It was a winter's day in February, 1646. Samuel Rutherford,
as we have seen, was then in London where he had been for
the past three years as one of the four Scottish commissioners
to the Westminster Assembly of Divines. Hopes had run
high when he, accompanied by his wife, Jean, and their two
small children, had first arrived in the English capital. But
the years had been hard. Long hours of protracted discus-
sions, sometimes with sharp disagreements, the loss of both
his children, coupled with his own indifferent health had left
Rutherford dispirited and weary. And now there came news
of the death of his much valued friend and correspondent,
Lady Boyd.

Picking up his pen Rutherford began to write a letter of
consolation to Lady Helen Ardross, his friend's daughter in
whose home she had died. 'She is now above the winter, with
a little change of place, not of a Saviour; only she enjoyeth
Him now without messages, and in His own immediate
presence, from whom she heard by letters and messengers
before.'

Lady Boyd's life had spanned more than seventy years and
from early days she had walked faithfully with her God: 'Ye
may easily judge, Madam,' Rutherford continued, 'what a
large recompense is made to all her service, her walking with
God, and her sorrows, with the first cast of the soul's eye
upon the shining and admirably beautiful face of the Lamb.'

As Rutherford contemplated the blessedness of her state he longed to enter into it himself. 'Certainly the hope of it, when things look so dark-like on both kingdoms, must be an exceeding great quickening to languishing spirits, who are far from home while we are here.'[1]

Samuel Rutherford had held Lady Boyd in highest regard, sharing fully in John Livingstone's estimate of her as 'a rare pattern of Christianity, grave, diligent and prudent'.[2] Only a few months earlier he had written to her from London describing some of the difficulties he was facing: 'We are here debating, with much contention of disputes, for the just measures of the Lord's temple. It pleaseth God, that sometimes enemies hinder the building of the Lord's house; but now friends, even gracious men . . . do not a little hinder the work.' The Reformation in Scotland had been thorough-going and deep, and so to Lady Boyd he now complained, 'For my part, I often despair of the reformation of this land . . . for the truth is, the best of them almost have said, "A half-reformation is very fair at the first;" which is no other thing than, "It is not time yet to build the house of the Lord."'[3]

Lady Boyd, whose maiden name was Christian Hamilton, was the only daughter of Sir Thomas Hamilton of Priestfield. Brilliant and distinguished, Sir Thomas' legal career had led him eventually to the honoured position of Keeper of the Privy Seal. By the time he was created Earl of Haddington in 1627, he had amassed huge wealth and was reputed to be one of the richest men of his day. But despite the lure of worldly honours, Christian Hamilton had a heart set on heavenly treasure and her renown lay in a life of godliness rather than the passing accolades of high society.

Shortly after the death of her first husband in 1616, Christian was married to Lord Robert Boyd. Seven children were born to them, but Lady Boyd was widowed a second time when Lord Robert died eleven years later in 1628. In addition, Lady Boyd lived in hard days for the true Church, days when 'they that feared the Lord spoke often one to another' to stimulate and encourage one another and many banded themselves into small praying groups to lay hold on God for His mercy. Lady Boyd was often present at such occasions in her area and when circumstances prevented her from attending, she set aside that time for personal prayer and fasting. Gatherings like these were to become the forerunners of the Conventicles of the persecution era when, hidden in many a mountain glen under the shadow of death, Christian men and women rejoiced together in the pure truths of the Word of God. Even in Lady Boyd's day they were frowned upon by the bishops and regarded as subversive.

In Northern Ireland the practice had been equally widespread, and during the intense persecution that drove men like Robert Blair back to Scotland, numbers of other Christians also came across and settled, particularly near Stirling. These small gatherings for fellowship then multiplied but some abuses also became apparent. Andrew Stevenson describes the situation: 'Some Brownists [as the early Independents were called] having got in amongst them found access, by degrees, for some of their conceits as forsaking the approved public worship of the congregation, discussing of curious and impertinent questions and censuring or slighting others of the godly as less holy than themselves.'[4]

Legislation finally came before the General Assembly in 1640 to outlaw all such private gatherings. Lady Boyd must have followed events with deep concern, fearful lest in an attempt to correct a fault, spiritual harm should result. The discussion was heated, in the fashion of the day, but one known to be an ardent upholder of church discipline vigorously defended them. It was Samuel Rutherford. A compromise was eventually hammered out, allowing the meetings to continue but imposing stricter controls on numbers and on those permitted to officiate.

We do not know when Rutherford first met Christian Boyd. Perhaps it was at a communion season or even at Kenmure Castle, but aware of her support for those suffering persecution, it was to her he directed one of his earliest letters from Aberdeen. He was troubled: had God rejected his service? had he been unfaithful? was he guilty of neglect in his ministry? These and other perplexing thoughts he confided to Lady Boyd.

Frequently Lady Boyd used her resources to support and encourage preachers of the gospel. Many received generous hospitality at her Kilmarnock home, near Glasgow: Robert Bruce, Robert Blair and John Livingstone among them. In his *Characteristics*, Livingstone records a fascinating detail of Lady Boyd's life, obviously noted on one such visit. 'She used every night to write what had been the case of her soul all the day long, and what she had observed of the Lord's dealings.'[5] The diary is lost or perhaps still lies yellowed with age in some forgotten chest of family papers. Night after night, sitting in her silent room, Lady Boyd would meditate on the day's events and seek to trace God's hand in all her circumstances. Often she was puzzled, sometimes disturbed, for her conscience was tender. So she wrote to Samuel Rutherford and in the ten letters he sent to her in reply, we have many indications of what the diary may have contained.

From early days Lady Boyd had been sensitive over aspects of her thoughts or conduct that might bring displeasure to God. A letter to Robert Boyd of Trochrig, cousin of her second husband, is typical of her spirit: 'O that anything would chase me to my God . . . When I should pray or read God's word or hear it preached or read, then my mind is possessed with thoughts how to avoid temporal grief, and how to get temporal contentment.'[6] To such problems Rutherford addressed himself in his letters. 'Now, Madam, for your Ladyship's case. . . . ,' he would write and then continue, 'Fear not, Christ will not cast water upon your smoking coal . . . He delighteth to take up fallen bairns, and to mend broken brows . . . Many a whole soul is in heaven which was sicker than ye are.'[7]

One problem frequently troubled Lady Boyd: some days she might experience an awareness of Christ's presence and then, inexplicably it would seem, her soul appeared barren, His nearness and blessings withdrawn. To this matter Rutherford returned again and again in his correspondence. It is one of the themes he dwells on at length in several of his other major writings, most notably *Christ Dying and Drawing Sinners to Himself*.[8] His teaching on the subject can be summed up in a few short words written to Lady Boyd, 'Hiding of His face is wise love.' Knowing how often she was baffled by such circumstances, he continues, 'Nay, His bairns must often have the frosty cold side of the hill, and set down both their bare feet among thorns. His love hath eyes, and, in the meantime, is looking on. Our pride must have winter weather to rot it.'[9]

One matter that weighed on Rutherford's mind during his Aberdeen confinement was the circumstances of his own brother George, a school teacher in Kirkcudbright. Shortly after Rutherford's exile, his brother was also summoned before the Courts to answer a charge of non-conformity. George was then ordered to resign his post and to move from Kirkcudbright within a few months. Unable to give him any assistance himself, Samuel Rutherford frequently mentioned his brother's needs in his letters. Lady Boyd was quick to help, for George had taken refuge in Ayrshire. Rutherford was grateful to her: 'I think myself many ways obliged to your Ladyship for your love to my afflicted brother, now embarked with me in that same cause. I hope that your Ladyship will befriend him with your counsel and countenance in that country where he is a stranger.'[10]

Lady Boyd experienced much sorrow in life. Twice she sustained the grief of widowhood and faced the formidable task of bringing up her numerous family alone. Both her sons – John, child of her first marriage, and Robert – warmly embraced the truths of biblical religion. They were among the thousands who subscribed to the National Covenant in Greyfriars Church, Edinburgh, in February 1638. Her daughters lived through the baptism of fire endured by the Covenanting Church of Jesus Christ in the reigns of Charles II and James II. One daughter, also named Christian, wife of Sir William Scot of Harden, employed the youthful Richard Cameron in 1675 as tutor to her family. Cameron, newly converted and with heart aflame for Christ, was soon to become one of the last leaders of the 'hill-men', as the Covenanter remnant was called. Perhaps she learnt from his lips to be courageous for truth, cost what it may. Certainly her unwillingness to compromise involved her husband in exorbitant and crippling fines. Writing of Lady Boyd's children many years earlier, Rutherford was able to say, 'Your Ladyship is blessed with children who are honoured to build up Christ's waste places again. I believe that your Ladyship will think them well bestowed on that work, and that Zion's beauty is your joy.'[11]

Further afflictions awaited Lady Boyd in her family circumstances. In 1640, three of her brothers and other relatives were killed when part of Dunglass Castle which they were defending against the invading English forces was mischievously blown up by a peevish English page boy. A group of about seventy men were standing near one of the castle walls, listening as Lady Boyd's brother, Thomas, second Earl of Haddington, read out a letter from General Leslie, who had marched on with the Covenanter forces further into England. Just before this, Edward Paris, the Earl's page boy, had been highly provoked because his master had mocked him calling the English a pack of cowards for running before General Leslie's men. Taking a red-hot poker, he thrust it angrily into a keg of gunpowder in the vault of the castle. In the subsequent explosion, the wall collapsed, killing all but a handful of the men standing nearby.

The circumstances of this incident were hard for Lady Boyd to accept, but Rutherford, writing from St Andrews, points her away from her troubled thoughts to the sovereign overruling hand of God. 'It is impossible to be submissive . . . if ye stay your thoughts down among the confused rollings and wheels of second causes; as, "Oh the place!" "Oh the time!" "Oh if this had been, this had not followed!" . . . Look up to the master-motion and the first wheel. See and read the decree of Heaven and the Creator of man.' Then with typical Rutherford imagery, he adds, 'I hope you have resolved that, if He should grind you to powder, your dust and powder will believe His salvation.'[12]

Only three months after this, young Robert Boyd died of a fever at the age of twenty-four. Rutherford had held out high hopes of this young man. 'I am glad to hear that you, in the morning of your short day, mind Christ, and that you love the honour of His crown and kingdom,' he had written several years earlier. Robert's spiritual zeal suggests he heeded Rutherford's further exhortations: 'Howbeit ye be a young flower . . . ye know not how soon death will cause you cast your bloom, and wither . . . therefore, write up what ye have to do for Christ, and make a treasure of good works and begin in time.'[13]

After these sorrows, Lady Boyd's pilgrim days were nearly done and in 1646 she was granted at last the uninterrupted enjoyment of her Saviour's presence for which she had longed. Robert Trail, minister of the parish of Elie, often visited her at Ardross Castle during her last illness and reported that she 'died comfortably'. Her death coincided with the end of the parliamentary session at nearby St

Andrews and many members of Parliament were glad of the opportunity to attend her funeral.

'I grant that death is to her a very new thing,' wrote Samuel Rutherford from London, 'but heaven was prepared of old. And Christ . . . is to her a new thing, but so new as the first summer-rose; . . . or as a new paradise to a traveller, broken and worn out of breath with the sad occurrences of the way.'[14]

8

Alexander Gordon: Witnessing a Good Confession

Earlston Castle – Private. This forbidding notice greets the motorist as he travels along a winding road near New Galloway in south-west Scotland. But to the intrepid the long tree-lined avenue leads to a handsome nineteenth century home where directions are readily given to the old castle, lying about half a mile beyond. Here, substantial but desolate, stands the family home of the Gordons of Earlston, bearing its silent testimony to the faith and endurance of former days.

Alexander Gordon, friend and correspondent of Samuel Rutherford, came from honourable lineage both in earthly and in spiritual terms. The Gordons of Lochinvar were a powerful and influential family in seventeenth century Scotland but Alexander had received a spiritual heritage from his fathers that far outweighed the temporal. This may be traced back four generations to the days when deep spiritual darkness rested across the land and the power of Rome held universal sway over the minds of the people. One man dared to challenge the religious system – a young man recently returned from Luther's Germany with the evangelical truths of the grace of God warm in his heart. This was Patrick Hamilton and Rome knew of only one way to deal with such a man: burn him. But signatures of leading members of the community must be obtained before such a sentence could be carried out and young Gordon of Airds, the great-grandfather of Rutherford's friend, was compelled to sign. So in 1528 a blameless youth, twenty-four years of age, was cruelly burnt at the stake in St Andrews. The very spot may still be seen marked with the initials P.H. in the pavement outside St Salvator's College. The repercussions of such an act were far other than Rome intended and led to popular indignation and quickened interest in the truths for which Hamilton died.

Gordon of Airds, shocked and ashamed, began to investigate Hamilton's beliefs and before very long, while trading across the English border, he discovered and bought a copy of Wycliffe's English New Testament. It was life-transforming. Soon Gordon, known as Strong Sandy for his exceptional physique, gathered others together and in the quiet woods surrounding his family home at Airds read the forbidden book to his tenants and neighbours. He revered its truths to the end of his long life (for he lived to be a hundred and one), and daily taught his family from its pages. Tradition tells us that the New Testament was found hidden within the walls of the castle when days of persecution were at last over.

Sandy Gordon's marriage to Margaret of Earlston united the family estates of Airds and Earlston and the truths honoured in that home were formative for generations to come. Alexander Gordon, great-grandson of Sandy, followed in that same noble tradition of faith and godliness. John Livingstone's pithy comments on Christians of his day form our best source of information on many of these men and women. He tells us of Alexander Gordon of Earlston that he was 'a man of great spirit but much subdued by inward exercise and one who attained the most rare experiences of downcasting and uplifting.'[1] Possibly imperious and stormy by birth, Alexander Gordon was a man whose passionate nature had been subdued by the grace of God. 'Humility is a strange flower,' said Samuel Rutherford on one occasion; 'it grows best in winter weather and under storms of affliction.'[2] This had been Gordon's experience. Through trial and sorrow, God had tamed Gordon's spirit and made him as a little child.

It was in July 1636 that Samuel Rutherford first wrote to Alexander Gordon. With his own ministry under threat from the Bishop of Galloway, Rutherford now wrote to encourage Gordon in the opposition he too was facing from the bishop: 'Ye are the first man in Galloway called out and questioned for the name of Jesus . . . Christ hath said, "Alexander Gordon shall lead the ring in witnessing a good confession," and therefore He hath put the garland of suffering for Himself first on your head.'[3]

The problems of patronage (the system that places the appointment of ministers into the hands of rich landowners or ecclesiastics, overriding the wishes of local congregations) have vexed good men through many years of Scottish church history and Alexander Gordon was a prototype of other Christians who later opposed such a system. The Bishop of Glasgow had summoned him before the Court of High Commission in 1633 because he had prevented the introduction of the bishop's nominee, unacceptable to the people, into a vacant parish near his estates. His eldest son, William, was to suffer for the same principle in later years. On this occasion the future Marquis of Argyll, Lady Kenmure's brother, intervened on Gordon's behalf and the matter was dropped. Not content that Gordon should escape so lightly, the Bishop of Galloway raised the same matter a year or two later and this was the occasion of the persecution to which Rutherford refers. Fined heavily and banished from his home, Alexander Gordon must have read over many times the words of Rutherford's letter: 'Suspend your reckoning till nigh the evening. Reckon not from the forenoon . . . howbeit body, life, and goods go for Christ your Lord, and though ye should lose the head for Him, yet there shall not one hair of your head perish; in patience therefore possess your soul.'[4] In the event, the order of banishment was dropped, but the heavy fine remained.

Ten years before these events John Livingstone, then but a young man of twenty-four, had visited Galloway and met Alexander Gordon of Earlston. He described him at that time as a 'worthy and experienced Christian', and later was to say, 'For wisdom, courage and righteousness he might have been a magistrate in any part of the earth.'[5] And this was the man that the opponents of true religion harassed, fined and persecuted. The signing of the National Covenant brought a temporary respite and Alexander Gordon became a member of the historic General Assembly of the Church that met in Glasgow during November of that year. With gladness, but not without fear of reprisal, the Reformation principles of worship and church order were re-established once more in the Scottish churches.

Even during that same July in 1636, when faced with the outward trial of persecution, Gordon also knew an inner desolation of spirit as several of his children were snatched away by death. 'If ye were not Christ's wheat, appointed to be bread in His house, He would not grind you,' Rutherford wrote to console his friend. Both his own children had died in infancy so it is with added poignancy that Rutherford could say, 'Thank God that Christ came to your house in your absence, and took with Him some of your children. He presumed that much on your love that ye would not offend . . . Ye see your Father is homely with you. Strokes of a father evidence kindness and care; take them so.'[6]

The sufferings of Alexander Gordon are written up in the chronicles of the times and preserved to posterity, but no word survives to tell of the sorrows that Lady Earlston knew as her children were taken from her in death or her husband wrongfully arraigned before the Church Courts. But Samuel Rutherford was not unmindful of her needs. Perhaps her griefs had broken her spirit, for Rutherford is not sure that all is well with her. 'I exhort you to go on in your journey; your day is short and your afternoon sun will soon go down,' he warns and then adds, 'Hurt not your conscience with any known sin.' The loss of her children was an affliction hard to be borne and Rutherford continues kindly, 'Let your children be as so many flowers borrowed from God: if the flower die and wither, thank God for the summer loan of them . . . Set your heart upon heaven, and trouble not your spirit with this clay-idol of the world.' Though he must warn and even rebuke Lady Earlston, he is in no real doubt of her sure standing in grace and concludes his letter with a prayer for her: 'The great Messenger of the Covenant, the Son of God, establish you on your Rock, and keep you to the day of His coming.'[7]

One last letter survives that Rutherford wrote to Alexander Gordon nearly ten years after the other seven. The former was in London at the time where the long task of drawing up the Westminster Confession of Faith was nearing completion. Clearly he was weary of dingy London streets and thought longingly of home and friends. Marion M'Naught and Lady Boyd had both died in recent years and Rutherford's mind often turned to 'Immanuel's highest land', true home of his soul. Alexander Gordon, now elderly, must be nearly there, he thought, and so he writes: 'If ye be near the water-side (as I know ye are) all that I can say is this, sir, that I feel by the smell of that land which is before you, that it is a goodly country . . . And He is before you, who will heartily welcome you.'[8] Alexander Gordon was sometimes disposed to faint or feel the life of faith almost too hard, so Rutherford writes this last letter to console him in the way. Tradition tells us that in his declining years Gordon was afflicted with a condition that robbed him of all power of movement until he was unable even to feed himself. Yet this great-spirited man had so long been subdued by inward exercise that daily, before his meals were fed to him by his wife, he would repeat Psalm 131, 'Surely I have behaved and quieted myself as a child that is weaned of his mother: my soul is even as a weaned child.' This became known as 'Alexander Gordon's grace before meat'.

Christ too was a sufferer, Rutherford assures his friend in this letter, and many of His people must tread that same hard path. But the believer's prospects compensate for all. There may be 'rubs in the way', but these are of little importance when 'the lodging is so good'. With these words he commits Alexander Gordon's soul into Christ's hand and so these fellow-sufferers part for a time, soon to be reunited for ever.

9

William Gordon:
Destitute, Afflicted, Tormented

A monument more than seven feet in height stands in the old churchyard in Glassford, near Glasgow. This memorial marks the place where a few frightened Covenanters, fugitives from the disastrous defeat of Bothwell Bridge in 1679, had buried the mortal remains of William Gordon of Earlston. Ruthlessly shot by the victorious king's dragoons, William Gordon was set free at last from the prison house of his sufferings into the pure air of heaven. Meanwhile the dragoons remounted and thundered off on their murderous way, caring little for any of these things.

It was even as Samuel Rutherford had written to William Gordon forty-two years earlier, when Gordon was little more than a teenager: 'The Lord's hopeful prisoners, under their trials, are in that case. Years and months will take out, now one little stone, then another, of this house of clay; and at length time shall win out the breadth of a fair door, and send out the imprisoned soul to the free air in heaven.'[1]

William was the eldest son of Alexander Gordon of Earlston, and from early days had served his apprenticeship in the school of persecution for Christ's sake. He was indeed a worthy son of such a father and the four letters that Samuel Rutherford wrote to this young man in 1637 bear testimony to the spiritual zeal and depth of Christian experience he had already attained at so early an age.

Christians living in days far removed from the seventeenth

century may perhaps think that a life of persecution is the exception rather than the norm; but it was not always so. 'I am persuaded,' wrote Samuel Rutherford to William Gordon, 'that it is a piece of the chief errand of our life . . . that we might suffer here for a time amongst our enemies; otherwise He might have made heaven to wait on us, at our coming out of the womb, and have carried us home to our country, without letting us set down our feet in this knotty and thorny life.'[2] These men expected a life of suffering and looked with anticipation, even with yearning desire, for a better world. 'O day, O fair day, O everlasting summer day, dawn and shine out, break out from under the black night sky, and shine!'[3]

Such a letter must have grown tattered and worn with constant re-reading as William Gordon faced unwarranted harassment and continual trial throughout his life. His name appears again and again in the records of the times, first on one charge, then on another, but always on issues where compromise would have meant a denial of the truths of the Reformation handed down from father to son and personally appropriated by each of the Gordons of Earlston.

Gabriel Semple was one of the early Covenanting preachers to take to the fields after the Act of 1663, known as the 'Bishop's Drag-Net', prohibiting Conventicles or field meetings. It was he who often came to the Woods of Airds and there, hidden among the dense foliage, he would preach to eager and attentive congregations. But someone informed on these outlawed gatherings and it was William Gordon who felt the stinging lash of persecution for his refusal to comply with the demand of the Council that he should not attend such meetings or allow them to be held on his land. A heavy fine with an order of banishment followed and although William Gordon probably did not leave the country for long, he certainly had to go into hiding.

Deep in the woods William Gordon and his family built a

small 'bolt-hole'. Here they escaped whenever the king's dragoons came to search for them. Sometimes, if insufficient warning were given, the leafy branches of a friendly oak growing near the house provided a quick hiding place. An old oak, perhaps the very tree, gnarled and broken by age and storm can still be seen not far from the castle. At last in 1667 the family home was ransacked and turned into a garrison for the king's marauding troops. From here the infamous Sir William Bannantyne conducted his cruel raids on the innocent peasantry of Galloway, intimidating, robbing and even torturing at times. We do not know where William Gordon and his family hid during that period. Perhaps the dark, damp hiding place in the woods became a more permanent shelter: it was never discovered, though many a search must have been made to find its whereabouts.

Nothing but a faith solidly grounded on the truths of Scripture and written indelibly in the heart by God Himself could enable a man to endure the spoiling of his goods with such steadfast courage as did William Gordon. It was this faith that drew the heart of Samuel Rutherford to him in early years and enabled the exiled pastor to say, 'I received your letter, which refreshed my soul.'[4] The friendship and concern shown by the older man must have been a source of strength in the dark and troubled days of Gordon's life. His letters are filled with his discoveries of Christ's goodness to those called upon to suffer for Christ's sake: 'Sweet, sweet is the cross of my Lord. The blessing of God upon the cross of my Lord Jesus! My enemies have contributed (beside their design) to make me blessed. This is my palace, not my prison.'[5] And again, 'Come all crosses, welcome, welcome! so that I may get my heartful of my Lord Jesus.'[6]

The uncommon candour with which Rutherford was able to share his spiritual experiences with a man many years his junior shines out in the four letters he wrote to William. 'Nay, verily, I was a child before . . . I would I could begin to be a Christian in sad earnest . . . But the truth is, for all my sorrow, Christ is nothing in my debt, for comforts have refreshed my soul.' And a little later in the same letter he confesses, 'I never took it to be so hard to be dead to my lusts and to this world.'[7] Such honesty must have encouraged a young Christian struggling with his failures but still longing for Christ's felt presence.

There is scarcely a more penetrating yet heartening letter in the whole collection than the one written to William Gordon on June 16, 1637. Having warned his correspondent of the spiritual dangers of youth, Rutherford packs this long letter with counsel, consolation and challenge. It would seem that Gordon had written a letter full of spiritual complaints and problems and Rutherford deals patiently and methodically with them one by one, adding with a touch of humour, 'He that can tell his tale, and send such a letter to heaven as he hath sent to Aberdeen, it is very like he will come speed with Christ.'[8] Sinful thoughts, a sense of unworthiness leading to loss of assurance, the hiding of Christ's face and the distinction between justification and sanctification are all carefully answered with scriptural argument. 'All Christ's good bairns go to heaven with a broken brow, and with a crooked leg,'[9] Rutherford had written, and this letter has brought relief to many another anxious believer since William Gordon's day.

'Oh, if our faith could ride it out against the high and proud waves and winds, when our sea seemeth to be all on fire!'[10] Rutherford had written to William Gordon, for he knew that his own sufferings were but the beginning of sorrows for Christians in Scotland. And it was only because Gordon's faith was firmly cast on the Rock that it survived the storm. By 1679 eighteen years of relentless persecution had decimated the Church of Jesus Christ in Scotland and a scattered suffering remnant had taken to desperate measures to try and throw off the tyrannical yoke of oppression. The

Battle of Bothwell Bridge was perhaps one of the saddest scenes enacted in the annals of that troubled era. Its stories of heroism coupled with tragedy, as a divided leadership among the Covenanters blew the trumpet with uncertain sound, can only arouse pity and sorrow in the reader. It was a vain stand, doomed to disaster, and led to an increase in the sufferings of the Covenanters as cruel reprisals followed their ignominious defeat. Perhaps William Gordon sensed that this was his last battle. Certainly he sent his son Alexander ahead of him to join the Covenanter forces while he himself put his affairs in order and followed later. Alexander narrowly escaped death by speedily borrowing a peasant woman's clothes and rocking her infant's cradle while the angry dragoons passed by, killing all who had been at the ill-fated battle scene. William never reached Bothwell Bridge but as he neared the spot, fleeing Covenanters must have told him that all was over. So he died, where the dragoons found him, shot without mercy, and his body was kicked into a ditch. There perished one described by John Howie in these words: 'a gentleman of good parts and endowments; a man devoted unto religion and godliness . . . a patriot, a good Christian, a confessor, and, I may add, a martyr of Jesus Christ.'[11]

It is well that these Covenanters looked confidently to a better world, for their earthly lot was one of continual deprivation, loss, injustice and pain. 'Our waters are but ebb, [shallow] and come neither to our chin, nor to the stopping of our breath. I may see (if I would borrow eyes from Christ) dry land, and that near,' wrote Samuel Rutherford to William Gordon those many years ago, and then continued, 'Why then should we not laugh at adversity, and scorn our short-born and soon-dying temptations?'[12] So William Gordon's storm-tossed vessel came at last to that 'dry land'. Now he could enter into those joys that Rutherford had anticipated long before as he looked beyond the things of time on into eternity: 'O Fairest among the sons of

SAMUEL RUTHERFORD AND HIS FRIENDS

men, why stayest Thou so long away? O heavens, move fast!
O time, run, run, and hasten the marriage day! for love is
tormented with delays . . . O blessed spirits who now see
His face, set Him on high! for when ye have worn your harps
in His praises, all is too little, and is nothing, to cast the smell
of the praise of that fair Flower, the fragrant Rose of Sharon,
through many worlds.'[13]

George Gillespie:
That Noble Youth

Nestling in the woods high above the still waters of Loch Ken, near New Galloway, stand the ruins of Kenmure Castle. The drive leading to the castle is damp and dark with overgrown foliage. But even this, with its eerie stillness, scarcely prepares the visitor for the sight that greets him as he climbs up to the desolate and roofless shell. The original thirteenth century structure was rebuilt in 1560 but suffered extensive fire damage at the hands of Cromwell's men in 1650. Since then each succeeding age has left its own stamp on the castle. Its massive stone walls are now clad in rough-cast with plaster-work interior. Nineteenth century sash windows, a 1920s telephone fixture and a chimney pot crowned with a present-day television aerial complete the bewildering scene. It was at Kenmure Castle, home of Sir John and Lady Kenmure and then a stately mansion, that Samuel Rutherford and George Gillespie were to meet.

Drawn from widely differing backgrounds Rutherford and Gillespie were of kindred spirit and we can well imagine the two men walking along the wooded banks of Loch Ken so deep in conversation that they scarcely noticed the beauty of their surroundings. George was the son of John Gillespie, minister of the gospel in Kirkcaldy, just north of Edinburgh, a man John Livingstone describes as 'a thundering preacher'. From earliest days George, who was born in 1613, was schooled in the things of God and his seriousness of disposition, coupled with an acute mind, soon marked him out as one whom God was preparing for particular usefulness in a day of much political and religious uncertainty. After a distinguished academic career at the University of St Andrews, Gillespie wished to enter the ministry. The depth of his convictions, however, seemed an insuperable obstacle, for he refused to be ordained at the hands of a bishop whose function in the Church he could not acknowledge. This effectively barred Gillespie's way into the ministry, for the bishops held positions of supreme power in the Church at that time. Yet it was these very circumstances that led to the forging of this lifelong bond with Samuel Rutherford, for in 1634 Gillespie came as chaplain to Lord and Lady Kenmure at Kenmure Castle. It was in that same year that Lord Kenmure died – a man whose dying words were to amaze and humble men for generations to come after they were published by Samuel Rutherford in 1649. George Gillespie would surely have witnessed, at least in part, that death-bed scene and heard words he could never forget.

Often must Rutherford, his pastoral duties completed, have sought out the company of young George Gillespie. The thirteen-year difference in their ages seemed as nothing, as their hearts burned in a common love for the truth of God in its purity and power. They were one in a desire for theological exactitude born of deep conviction of the truth; they read the same books and shared the same burdens for the troubles of the Church of Jesus Christ and for the sorrows of Christian men and women suffering for their uncompromising convictions. More than this, the same devotion to the person of the Son of God bound them in union one with the other. Both men faced a hazardous future as the iron grip of the bishops tightened on men of the stamp of Rutherford and Gillespie. Little wonder then that these two should establish a lifelong friendship in those short months they spent together in Galloway.

Soon after the death of Lord Kenmure came the time when Gillespie was to leave the castle to take up a chaplaincy with the Earl of Cassilles. Before leaving those peaceful woods surrounding the stately castle, it would appear that Rutherford and Gillespie committed themselves one to another and to God in a solemn covenant of friendship and prayer. Like David and Jonathan long ago, their hearts were knit together in a deep spiritual affinity and we can well imagine them kneeling together and undertaking always to pray for one another and to share the dealings of God with their souls. It was a covenant which would outlast even Gillespie's early death some fourteen years later and extend in concern for his widow and family.

Only three letters, two written from Aberdeen, survive to bear witness to the quality of friendship Rutherford and Gillespie enjoyed. 'Brother, remember our old covenant, and pray for me, and write to me your case,'[1] Rutherford urges. He is able to confide to the younger man the fears and vacillations of faith that distressed him during the early weeks of his exile. 'At my first entry, my apprehensions so wrought upon my cross, that I became jealous of the love of Christ, as being by Him thrust out of the vineyard, and I was under great challenges . . . ' but Christ delivered him from this state of temptation, and now he exclaims joyfully, 'I want little of half a heaven, and I find Christ every day, so sweet, comfortable, lovely, and kind.'[2]

While Rutherford served his God by suffering in His cause, Gillespie took up his pen and wrote a treatise called *A Dispute against the English Popish Ceremonies*. Although he was scarcely twenty-five years of age, the ability demonstrated in this work immediately established for George Gillespie a reputation that was to become a legend even in his short life-span. 'I admire the man though I mislike much of his matter,' admitted his contemporary, Robert Baillie, rather grudgingly, in reference to this work. 'Yea, I think he may prove among the best wits of this isle.'[3]

The triumphs of 1638, with the signing of the National Covenant and the curbing of the powers of the bishops, at last allowed George Gillespie to take up the work nearest to his heart and enter the Christian ministry as pastor of the church at Wemyss, near Glasgow. He was ordained in April of that year, being the first man to receive ordination in that period without the official acknowledgement of the bishops. His zeal for the truth was further demonstrated by a sermon preached at the historic Assembly of the Church in 1638 following the signing of the Covenant. It was entitled 'The King's heart is in the hand of the Lord', and so compelling were his arguments that his friends feared the consequence of such bold preaching. The Marquis of Argyll, Lady Kenmure's brother, supported by the Moderator, Alexander Henderson, cautioned the young preacher and suggested that his comments could well inflame the situation and further arouse the anger of the king against his northern subjects.

In 1643 Rutherford and Gillespie were united once more as they worked side by side at the Westminster Assembly. Chosen as one of the four main Scottish representatives, Gillespie proved to be among the ablest theologians present, though only thirty years of age. His outstanding gifts as a debater and thinker were an invaluable asset in the long search for accurate expressions of scriptural truth.

Robert Baillie, also one of the Scottish commissioners, is glowing in his description of Gillespie's contribution. The reluctant praise of earlier days has been replaced by a whole-hearted admiration for Gillespie's God-given abilities. He speaks of him as 'very learned and acute Mr. Gillespie' and again as 'that noble youth, Mr. Gillespie' and adds, 'I truly admire his faculty and bless God . . . for him in that faculty with the first of the whole Assembly.'[4] The story is told of one occasion when with devastating brilliance Gillespie demolished all the Erastian arguments of their protagonist, John Selden. Selden, who had spent long years seeking to establish from ancient Rabbinical documents the supposed right of the monarch to supremacy in the Church, was heard to say with sorrowful chagrin, 'That youth has in a single speech swept away the learning and labour of ten years of my life.' When his friends crowded round to look at the notes of such a speech, they found only a few words scribbled on a scrap of paper, 'Give light, O Lord; O Lord, defend thine own cause'.[5]

On his return to Scotland, Gillespie was honoured to be elected Moderator of the General Assembly in 1648 but within a year of these events this promising young man lay dying, his frail constitution no longer able to support the passionate spirit. Rutherford was dumbfounded: the loss of such a friend at an hour of deepening crisis for the Church of Jesus Christ left him silent and amazed. 'I dare say nothing against His dispensation,' he wrote sorrowfully, 'I hope to follow quickly.'[6]

Though a man of exceptional spiritual qualities, George Gillespie found dying hard indeed. His problem lay not in an unwillingness to part with wife, family and friends, difficult though that was, for he was able to declare that he was longing to depart, but the 'last enemy' assaulted the dying man with unrelenting ferocity and in those final troubled months of his life he seemed to lose assurance of his acceptance before God. Sins and failures of past years rose up before his eyes with alarming clarity and the eternal city seemed veiled from sight.

At such a time Samuel Rutherford proved a friend indeed, both by his letters and the visits from St Andrews to Kirkcaldy where the sick man lay. As a true pastor, Rutherford knew well that constant introspection, when a man's spirit is low through physical weakness, could bring nothing but distress. Rather he urged his friend to turn his eyes away from his inadequacies to the Son of God. 'If ye look to yourself as divided from Christ, ye must be more than heavy,' he admonishes. Never has God required any more of a man than saving faith in order to account him righteous and so Rutherford persists, 'Be not heavy. The life of faith is now called for; *doing* was never reckoned in your accounts, though Christ in and by you hath done more than by twenty, yea, an hundred grey-haired and godly pastors.'[7] Such words must surely have brought relief to the conscience and enabled Gillespie to say, 'Though the Lord allow me no comfort, yet I will *believe* that my Beloved is mine and I am His.'[8]

'Would not Christ be a welcome guest to you now?' enquired Rutherford tenderly as he stood by his friend. 'The welcomest guest that ever I saw,' was the simple reply.[9] And so, protesting that it was 'reward enough that ever I got leave to do Him any service', George Gillespie exchanged the gloom and darkness of earth for the glories of the City of God.

All Scotland mourned his loss, and though only thirty-five years of age, he left behind an enduring testimony by both word and pen. Asked what advice he would give to other preachers, he said, 'I have little experience of the ministry . . . but I can say that I have got more assistance in the work of preaching by prayer than by study and more help from the assistance of the Spirit than from books.'[10] At Rutherford's request, only days before he died, he had dictated a solemn statement of the dangers facing the true Church of Jesus Christ. He urged others to be bold and unflinching in their allegiance to the truth, which 'if men will do . . . they shall see His work go on and prosper gloriously'.[11]

'Ye must leave the wife to a more choice Husband, and the children to a better Father,'[12] Rutherford had written when he learnt that his friend was dying. It is a tribute to the public esteem in which Gillespie was held that a gift of £1,000 was made to his widow by the Committee of Estates.

Grief followed on grief for this young woman, as only a few months later a little son, Archibald, followed his father to the grave and Rutherford wrote these moving words to the bereaved mother: 'I should wish that, at the reading of this, ye may fall down and make a surrender of those that are gone, and of those that are yet alive, to Him. And for you, let Him have all; and wait for Himself . . . He cannot die whose ye are.'[13]

Jean Brown, Lady Robertland and Barbara Hamilton: Far Above Rubies

'Who can find a virtuous woman?' asks the Book of Proverbs, 'for her price is far above rubies.'[1] Samuel Rutherford would have had little difficulty in pointing out a galaxy of women whose shining virtues of grace and godliness placed their worth 'far above rubies'. Lady Kenmure, Lady Boyd, Marion M'Naught and Lady Culross stand out in brightness from among the many 'ladies of the Covenant' with whom he corresponded, but only because more details of their lives have been preserved to posterity. A glance, however, at the index to the *Letters of Samuel Rutherford* reveals names of many other women about whom little is known and some who are merely addressed as 'a Christian gentlewoman'. It is immediately evident from these letters that some of these knew a degree of communion with Christ and a familiarity with the ways of God that is strangely rare in the Church of our day.

JEAN BROWN

Jean Brown was a friend of Marion M'Naught and probably lived in Kirkcudbright. On more than one occasion Rutherford asks Marion M'Naught to inform Jean Brown of his needs and solicits her prayers. She was the mother of the distinguished theologian and expositor, John Brown of Wamphray, whose writings Alexander Smellie describes as 'a library in themselves'.[2] Rutherford had long noticed the earnest disposition and uncommon ability of Jean Brown's lad and set his affections on him. 'I rejoice to hear that your son John is coming to visit Christ, and taste of His love,' he writes in a letter to Jean Brown and adds, 'I had always (as I said often to you) a great love to dear Mr John Brown, because I thought I saw Christ in him more than in his brethren.'[3] Again in a later letter to Marion M'Naught, he comments of John Brown, 'I never could get my love off that man: I think Christ hath something to do with him.'[4]

There was scarcely a family that did not experience its share of suffering for the sake of the truth in those days of intense religious intolerance and John Brown was but one of many able and gifted ministers ejected from his living and exiled to Rotterdam at the Restoration of Charles 11 to the throne in 1660. It was twenty-five years before these events that Rutherford was corresponding with Jean Brown, but it seems that each of the three letters written to John's mother was designed in God's purposes to forewarn her of the sufferings which she and her family must endure for Christ's sake.

All three of these letters were written during the early months of Rutherford's Aberdeen confinement and the last two within a week of each other. All follow a similar pattern: the brevity of life and the transitory nature of earthly joys contrasted with the enduring pleasures that await Christ's believing people. These were the lessons that Rutherford himself was learning in his bleak northern fortress and they are the dominating theme in many of the early letters he wrote. He anticipated, and rightly, a day of severe travail for the Church of Jesus Christ in Scotland. Christians must be prepared to endure to the end a burden of affliction that would prove too arduous for the many who merely professed to be believers: 'It is not the sunny side of Christ that we must look to,' he warns Jean Brown, 'but must set our face against what may befall us in following on, till He and we be through the briers and bushes, on the dry ground.'[5]

It is our worldly-mindedness that gives affliction its sting and Rutherford encourages Jean Brown in an evaluation of this life that will cast any degree of persecution into its right perspective. 'We smell of the smoke of this lower house of the earth, because our hearts and our thoughts are here,' he maintains. 'Our crosses would not bite upon us if we were heavenly-minded.'[6] It is the hope of glory that can nerve our faint-hearted faith and give us the strength to sustain the trial: 'Oh, what telling is in Christ!' he exclaims, 'Oh, how weighty is my fair garland, my crown, my fair supping-hall in glory! . . . Let this be your desire, and let your thoughts dwell much upon that blessedness that abideth you in the other world.'[7]

No mention is made of Jean Brown's husband and it is likely that he had already died. Samuel Rutherford is not unmindful of her difficulties in bringing up her family of boys alone. He has a special exhortation for her son Patrick: 'I desire Patrick to give Christ his young love, even the flower of it . . . It were good to start soon to the way; he should thereby have great advantage in the evil day.'[8] Nor does he forget the sense of isolation that Jean Brown must often have known and has a kindly word for her too: 'I commend Christ to you, as your last-living, and longest-living Husband, and the staff of your old age. Let Him now have the rest of your days. And think not much of a storm upon the ship that Christ saileth in.'[9]

It is evident from their correspondence that Jean Brown was one to whom Rutherford was prepared to commit some of the deepest longings of his heart after Christ and His manifest presence. We find these words entrusted to her: 'I am in as sweet communion with Christ as a poor sinner can be; and am only pained that HE hath much beauty and fairness, and *I* little love; HE great power and mercy, and *I* little faith; HE much light, and *I* bleared eyes.'[10] Yet even the highest spiritual experiences are marred both because this is a fallen world and because sin still lingers in the heart of a believer. 'Our joys here are born weeping, rather than laughing, and they die weeping,' says Rutherford in one of his quaint expressions. Rutherford knew nothing of the triumphalism that has too often characterized much of the interchange between Christians in other times. He is ruthlessly honest with himself and consequently able to help others who are conscious of spiritual failure. So he continues to Jean Brown, 'Sin, sin, this body of sin and corruption embittereth and poisoneth all our enjoyments. O that I were where I shall sin no more!'[11] This spiritual struggle sharpened the intensity of Rutherford's homesickness for 'our country above'. 'God keep our better home!' he exclaims to Jean Brown with earnest desire. The sufferings of a Christian should lead to a right estimate of this life and so he urges Jean Brown on in these words: 'I am sure that this is the best fruit of the cross, when we, from the hard fare of the dear inn, cry the more that God would send a fair wind, to land us, hungered and oppressed strangers, at the door of our Father's house.'[12]

We do not know whether Jean Brown lived to experience the storm of persecution that broke both on her family and on Christ's Church at the Restoration, but she must often have pondered upon Rutherford's words: 'Our sand-glass is not so long as we need to weary; time will eat away and root out our woes and sorrow. Our heaven is in the bud, and growing up to an harvest,'[13] and in that harvest both Jean Brown and Samuel Rutherford were soon to rejoice in full measure.

LADY ROBERTLAND

Lady Robertland, a resident in the Stewarton area of west

Scotland, was greatly used of God at a time of significant spiritual awakening. Numerous revivals had swept through those parts between the years 1625 and 1630 and Robert Fleming in his fascinating contemporary account describes the period as 'this great spring-tide of the Gospel'.[14] Many were powerfully converted, including numbers whose sole motive for attending the preaching initially was to deride it. More than this, the converts of this revival experienced so deep a work of God on their souls that the quality of their Christian lives subsequently became a by-word in the land. Even the godless Count of Eglintoun was compelled to admit, after speaking with some of these people, that 'he never spoke with the like of them and wondered at the wisdom they manifest in their speech'.[15]

Like every genuine work of the Spirit of God, the Stewarton revivals became 'a sign spoken against'. So profound were the convictions of sin among these people that Robert Fleming tells us, 'many were so choken and taken by the heart . . . the Spirit in such a measure convincing them of sin, in hearing of the word, they have been made to fall over, and thus carried out of the church; who afterward proved most solid and lively Christians.'[16] Some were inclined to mock, calling these physical reactions 'the Stewarton sickness', and described these people as 'the daft people of Stewarton'. It was, however, in these circumstances that Lady Robertland was especially used by God. Her home became a refuge for those seeking assurance of salvation and many in distress of soul found in this woman a true 'mother in Israel'.

It is evident that God had long been preparing Lady Robertland for this service. John Livingstone writes that she was 'one deeply exercised in her mind'.[17] Before she could point troubled souls to the Saviour, she herself had to be taught and must serve a severe apprenticeship in the ways of God. Samuel Rutherford wrote only one letter to Lady

Robertland but in it he is clearly referring to some of these things: 'I shall be glad to hear that your soul prospereth, and that fruit groweth upon you, after the Lord's husbandry and pains, in His rod that hath not been a stranger to you from your youth.' Few would find it easy to add an 'Amen' to the prayer that Rutherford pens as he concludes this letter, but after her experiences of God's dealings Rutherford knew that Lady Robertland could do so: 'Lord cut, Lord carve, Lord wound, Lord do anything that may perfect thy Father's image in us, and make us meet for glory.'[18] Even though she had learnt much in Christ's school, Rutherford assures her that none fully masters all He would teach in this life: 'We are still ill scholars and will go in at heaven's gates wanting the half of our lesson; and shall still be bairns, so long as we are under time's hand.'

Lady Robertland and Samuel Rutherford shared a similar cast of mind. Even her quaint manner of speech in which she continually pointed out parallels between the normal things of life and spiritual truths was akin to Rutherford's own graphic turn of mind. This one letter he wrote to her is packed with symbolic thought from start to finish, for he knew he wrote to one who would appreciate and understand it.

Not only was Lady Robertland deeply exercised in God's ways but she was one who obtained 'rare out-gates', so Livingstone records. By this expression he means that she had known extraordinary, even dramatic deliverances from God in times of trouble. Lady Robertland loved to talk of her 'rare out-gates' in order that her great Deliverer might be praised and it is evident from the letter Rutherford wrote that he was familiar with the stories of these remarkable providences. With typical imagery he turns the metaphor and says that Christ too has a secret gate by which he visits the souls of His people: 'He hath a gate of His own beyond the thoughts of men, that no foot hath skill to follow Him.' Not only has

Christ a secret gate but the keys also are in His sole possession: 'Christ keepeth the keys . . . If He would come in, I shall not dispute the matter, where He get a hole or how He opened the lock.' By this twist of imagery Rutherford was pointing Lady Robertland to the sovereignty of God in the visitations of grace to the hearts of His people.

This was needful for in spite of her unusual experiences, Lady Robertland suffered much from spiritual depression. Livingstone tells us that even as late as 1649, eleven years after Rutherford penned these words and twenty years after the Stewarton revivals, Lady Robertland could still be cast into the depths, losing all assurance of her acceptance before God. At such times it seemed as if Christ had hidden Himself far from her and then even life's smallest grievances became an intolerable burden. Emerging from such a period, she once declared to John Livingstone, '*With* Him the most of mosts is lighter than nothing; and *without* Him the least of leasts is heavier than any burden.'[19] Rutherford well understood such experiences, having frequently passed that way himself and often must his words of counsel have supported and encouraged Lady Robertland in her darkest moments: 'I see there is a sort of impatient patience required in the want of Christ as to His manifestations,' he writes and then explains himself: 'They thrive who wait on His love . . . and the turning of His gracious wind; and they thrive who, in that on-waiting, make haste and din and much ado for their lost and hidden Lord Jesus.'[20] Even though despair was never far away, one day, Rutherford assures her, the darkness will lift for ever and though now we may often 'spill and mar our own fair heaven, soon eternity [will] cause a sun to arise in our souls'.[21]

BARBARA HAMILTON

A strong hand gripped the arm of the Treasurer of the Privy

Council. A loud female voice declared, 'Stand, my Lord! in Christ's name, I charge you, till I speak to you.' Barbara Hamilton it was who spoke and the Treasurer had no option other than to pause and receive her request.

Barbara Hamilton was the sister of Beatrix, Robert Blair's first wife. The loss of such a wife as Beatrix had been a severe one, for she was a woman of gentle and amiable temperament and godly character. This was only the beginning of a succession of heavy trials for Robert Blair. In spite of the powerful work of the Spirit of God re-establishing Christianity in Ireland under the preaching of Blair, John Livingstone and William Cunningham, these men were removed from their spheres of usefulness and prohibited from further preaching by prelates opposed to biblical religion. After their abortive attempt to emigrate to New England in 1636, Blair returned to Belfast but was hounded out once more. Persecution followed him on his return to Scotland until this man of God was effectively silenced.

It was in 1637 that Blair's sister-in-law, Barbara Hamilton, intervened. With remarkable strength of purpose this intrepid woman organized and drew up a petition to be presented to the Privy Council on behalf of Blair and other preachers who had been treated in a similar way. Then she rallied as many of the like-minded women of Edinburgh as she could muster and lined them up from the door of the Council Chamber to the street. The petition itself was entrusted to the oldest of the women, as she imagined that in this way it would stand a greater chance of success. Barbara Hamilton was wrong. The Treasurer, seeing it was only an elderly lady who approached him, thrust her aside and tried to enter the Council Chambers. But he had not reckoned with Barbara Hamilton. At this moment she quickly took the petition from her friend and demanded the Treasurer's attention.

'Good woman, what would you say to me?' the Councillor asked nervously.

'There is a humble supplication of Mr Blair,' came the insistent reply. 'All that he petitions for is that he may have liberty to preach the Gospel. I charge you to befriend the matter, as you would expect God to befriend you in your distress and at your death.'

In the face of such words the Councillor had little alternative: 'I shall do my endeavour and what I can in it,' he replied, and disappeared thankfully inside. The petition was granted; Blair was able to take up his ministry once more and a future of eminent usefulness opened up before him. Such is the account of the initiative of this Deborah of the Scottish Church.[22] Undoubtedly Samuel Rutherford, imprisoned in Aberdeen, would have heard of the incident and noted her name.

We have seen Rutherford and Robert Blair closely connected through more than twenty years during their days at St Andrews. Samuel Rutherford would soon have gained a personal acquaintance with Blair's strong-minded sister-in-law and the more so because Barbara Hamilton's son-in-law, William Hume, was a promising young preacher who learnt his theology at the feet of Rutherford in St Mary's College of Divinity. Rutherford clearly knew William Hume well, for he describes him as 'your son-in-law and my friend' and held high hopes that he should exercise a long and successful ministry. But this was not to be. William Hume was killed in 1643 at Newcastle, where he was stationed as part of the Covenanter army that had joined the Parliamentary troops in the struggle against the Royalists. The sad irony was that William Hume was not killed by an enemy bullet but, it would appear, by a stray bullet from a gun in his own camp.

Samuel Rutherford was in London at the time and immediately he heard the news, he took up his pen to write both to Barbara Hamilton and to her daughter – now left a widow. In the letter to Barbara Hamilton he takes up the theme of the sovereignty of God as the first cause of all events. This the believer must humbly acknowledge and 'the hand which never did wrong, should be kissed and adored by us'.[23] His purposes are often beyond our understanding, for we see only the raw materials of His designs: 'We see red earth, unbroken clods, furrows and stones, but we see not summer lilies, roses, the beauty of a garden.' One purpose, however, we can understand and that is the work of sanctification for which afflictions are often designed. 'I know our Lord aimeth at more mortification; let Him not come in vain to your house, and lose the pains of a merciful visit. God, the Founder, never melteth in vain; howbeit to us He seemeth often to lose both fire and metal.'[24]

A month later, perhaps fearing that his former letter had not reached Barbara Hamilton, Rutherford wrote again developing these same themes. God is in control of events: He can never make mistakes and so 'When He was directing the bullet against His servant to fetch out the soul, no wise man could cry to God, "Wrong, wrong, Lord, for he is thine own!" There is no mist over His eyes who is "wonderful in counsel."'[25] It might seem inexplicable in earthly terms for 'Christ hath fewer labourers in His vineyard than He had', but the ministry that William Hume began on earth would be perfected in a better world. 'I know he now praiseth the grace he was to preach.'[26]

So Rutherford consoles Barbara Hamilton and when writing to the young widow, adds these words: 'Quietness, silence, submission, and faith, put a crown on your sad losses . . . Believe and submit; and refer the income of the consolations of Jesus, and the event of the trial, to your heavenly Father, who numbereth all your hairs.'[27] And even though none could fathom God's ways at that time, one fruit of the death of William Hume was surely these three letters of consolation written to Barbara Hamilton and her daughter that have brought many other grieving believers to acknowledge both the sovereignty and mercy of God in times of affliction.

12

John Livingstone and Lady Culross:
A Living Stone

John Livingstone was discouraged. It was 1631 and scarcely a year had elapsed since he had arrived at Killinchy, in County Down, Northern Ireland, as a preacher of the gospel. It had been a hard year, for the people were superstitious and untaught, but God had owned his labours: many had been converted and a strong church established. The Bishop of Down, however, viewed these developments with a jaundiced eye and now, upon some small pretext, had deposed Livingstone from his church. It was at this point that John Livingstone received a letter from his friend and correspondent, Lady Culross. Heading her letter with words from Psalm 76, 'The wrath of man shall praise thee,' she wrote, 'Courage, dear brother, all is in love, and works together for the best. You must be hewed and hammered down and prepared before you are a LIVING STONE fit for his building.'[1]

With this play on his name Lady Culross tried to encourage John Livingstone, whom she had known since a child. Born in 1603, John was one of a family of seven; his father, William Livingstone, had also been in the ministry, first at Kilsyth and then in Lanark. William and his wife Agnes delighted to give hospitality to Christians visiting their area, especially at communion seasons. In this way young John had the privilege of meeting a considerable number of the notable men and women of his day. This circumstance

ently back in Anwoth, hurried to Edinburgh and was among the first to sign. Rutherford, however, did not leave Aberdeen until June 1638, his last letter from there bearing the date June 11th. He himself makes no reference to the occasion, though we know from Robert Baillie's *Letters* that he preached in Glasgow that June, probably on his way back to Anwoth.[38] The most conclusive evidence, however, comes from a careful study of the original Covenant itself, now yellowed and worn and kept between glass plates in the Huntly House Museum in Edinburgh. Over four thousand signatures have been counted, many now blurred with age, but none appears to be Rutherford's. This is confirmed by Andrew Stevenson in his detailed and authoritative *History of the Church and State of Scotland* from 1625–1649, first published in three volumes between 1753 and 1757. Stevenson gives a comprehensive account of all events surrounding the signing of the Covenant, basing his work on early source material. Included in a footnote is a list of some of the better-known ministers who added their names that day. Rutherford's name is conspicuously absent.

Rumours of these momentous events, however, would have filtered through to Samuel Rutherford in Aberdeen – a city notorious for its affiliation to the Episcopal party. It must have added to his frustration and sense of uselessness if he were left on one side at such a time. But God was at work through it all giving His people at least temporary respite from the heavy hand of religious intolerance. A season of spiritual awakening spread throughout the land and once again the Church of Jesus Christ was clothed in the garments of praise instead of the spirit of heaviness. Robert Fleming in his contemporary account of those days says, 'Since the land was engaged by covenant to the Lord, what a solemn outletting of the Spirit hath been seen; a large harvest with much fruit of the Gospel discernible hath been proved in the inbringing of thousands to Christ.'[39]

The Episcopal party was much weakened by these events and Rutherford, deciding it was time to risk the fury of the law, discharged himself from exile. After an absence of nearly two years, Anwoth received its pastor back once more and gladness spread through castle and cottage alike. But it was not for long; within a year the General Assembly of the Church of Scotland expressed the wish that Samuel Rutherford become Professor of Divinity at St Mary's College in St Andrews. Rutherford's gifts could no longer be confined to Anwoth, but he was far from willing to comply with the Assembly's request. The memory of his recent 'dumb Sabbaths' was still too painful and in a letter to Lady Kenmure he complains ruefully: 'My removal from my flock is so heavy to me, that it maketh my life a burden to me; I had never such a longing for death. The Lord help and hold up sad clay.'[40] But Rutherford was compelled to yield to God's unmistakable will, not only to the larger blessing of Christ's Church but also to posterity, for his distance from Galloway ensured the continued correspondence with Lady Kenmure, Marion M'Naught and other friends.

St Andrews had a bad reputation. Robert M'Ward, who studied there under Rutherford, describes it as 'the very nursery of all superstition in worship and error in doctrine and the sink of all profanity in conversation among the students.' Rutherford gave himself to the work with 'unparalleled and holy zeal', M'Ward tells us. In addition to his lectures on theology, he also taught Hebrew and church history. Within a few years a marked change was apparent in St Andrews so that M'Ward could add this glowing comment: 'God did so signally second his servant's indefatigable pains . . . that it became forthwith a Lebanon out of which were taken cedars for building the house of the Lord through the whole land.'[41] Coupled with his academic work, Rutherford also assisted Robert Blair in the preaching in St Andrews, a concession he had gained as a prerequisite for equipped him in future years to compile his *Memorable Characteristics*, a work that has provided us with fascinating insights into the lives of his contemporaries.

Lady Culross was a regular visitor at the manse and perhaps noticed John's serious disposition and abilities. When he was fourteen, John's mother died; it was a bereavement hard to be borne for she was only thirty-two and her children still young. Livingstone describes his mother as 'a rare pattern of piety and meekness'.[2] Maybe Lady Culross tried to compensate in some way for the loss. Certainly the eight letters preserved for us that she wrote to John reveal the warm regard in which she held him.

Shortly after his mother's death John Livingstone went to the College of Glasgow, as the University was then known. Here he was privileged to study under Robert Blair, graduating in 1621. Early converted to God, Livingstone first began to preach in 1625. For a year he lived at home, gaining valuable experience as he preached at neighbouring churches. In 1626 he went to Galloway at the invitation of Sir John Gordon to preach there. No church building existed at Anwoth at the time and Sir John asked Livingstone to delay settling at a church until August, by which time he hoped to have a building erected. Livingstone was prepared to wait but there was a delay in the building project and in the meantime another opportunity appeared to be opening up for the young preacher. He comments with typical modesty, 'Thereafter the Lord provided a great deal better for them, for they got that worthy servant of Christ, Mr Samuel Rutherford, whose praise is in all the reformed churches.'[3] This was the time that Livingstone first met young Lady Jane Gordon and in his account of his life he includes a passing reference to her spiritual zeal. Nearly forty years later, lying on his death-bed far from Scottish shores, he mentions her again and with equal appreciation – a testimony to her faith in spite of a life of heavy affliction.

Although John Livingstone ministered acceptably in various places during the following four years, his final settlement in a church was continually blocked by the opposition of the prelates. But 1630 was to be a turning point in his life. It was on June 30 of that year that the revival at the Kirk o'Shotts took place. Referring to his preaching on that occasion, Livingstone says: 'I never preached a sermon that I would be in earnest to see again in writing but two: the one was the Monday after the Communion at Shotts and the other after the Communion at Holyrood, and both these times I spent the whole night before in conference and prayer with some Christians.'[4]

Lady Culross was among the small group of men and women who gave themselves to earnest intercession that Sunday night in Shotts. John Livingstone writes of her in these words: 'Of all that ever I saw she was the most unwearied in religious exercises; and the more she attained access to God therein, she hungered the more.'[5] Several well-known preachers had taken part during that weekend including David Dickson and Robert Bruce, now very elderly. The services had been accompanied by surprising manifestations of the presence of God and by Sunday evening the expectant people were unwilling to disperse.

A preacher was then approached and asked to address the people the next day, but he was subsequently taken ill, so at Lady Culross' suggestion, John Livingstone, only twenty-seven years of age and virtually unknown, was persuaded with considerable difficulty to fill his place. As this young man stood on a gravestone preaching to that vast concourse of people, God powerfully aided him by His Spirit. Just as he was about to conclude his message, heavy rain began to fall. People reached for their coats but remained transfixed. Fresh liberty was given to the preacher, who continued his sermon a further hour, demonstrating the horror and despair that must take hold of the unbelieving when the fire and brimstone of God's just judgments falls on them, and also exhorting the people to flee to Jesus Christ, the only refuge in that storm. The effect of such preaching was profound. Robert Fleming, a contemporary writer, informs us in his *Fulfilling of the Scriptures* that nearly five hundred 'had a discernible change wrought on them'[6] on that one day, and most of these proved their profession to be genuine throughout the remainder of their lives.

Following this revival, Lady Culross was anxious to secure Livingstone's services for her own church. But it was not to be, and she expressed her disappointment in a strongly worded letter when she heard of Livingstone's unexpected departure for Ireland. 'Your sudden voyage has troubled me more since than ever, and many of this congregation who would have preferred you to others . . . but now I fear the charm is spilt, yet you cannot go out of my mind . . .'[7]

Lady Culross had always taken delight in encouraging the Lord's servants. But when Livingstone faced difficulties in Ireland, she might well have been tempted to chide him again for his hasty departure. Instead, she says kindly, 'You write that you are likely to have no settling there. If God have a work for you to do there he can change hearts, if here, he can and will open a door, though never so fast closed . . . I fear that when you first went to Ireland that you did run too swiftly . . . but God has a work in all for his glory.'[8]

Nearly thirty years before these events, Lady Culross had written to John Welsh, minister of Ayr, to encourage him when he was imprisoned in Blackness, that notorious gaol where many Covenanters were to languish in future days. Possessed of considerable poetic gift, she composed some verses for him:

> Now it is dark, the sky cannot be clear,
> After the clouds it shall be calm anon.
> Wait on his will whose blood has bought thee dear;
> Extol his name though outward joys be gone.

> Look to the Lord, thou art not left alone;
> Since he is thine what pleasure can they take?
> He is at hand and hears thy every groan,
> End out thy fight and suffer for his sake.[9]

With the passing years, Lady Culross retained her concern for the persecuted people of God and when Samuel Rutherford was banished north to Aberdeen, it was Lady Culross who was the first to write to him. The freedom and honesty with which Rutherford replies to this letter demonstrates the high regard in which Lady Culross was held among her contemporaries. Writing from Edinburgh before leaving for Aberdeen, Rutherford is tending to blame himself for his circumstances but even so is able to rise above his depression and predicts: 'I know Christ shall make Aberdeen my garden of delights.'[10]

In the next letter that the exiled pastor wrote to Lady Culross, his faith has triumphed over his fears and he tells her of the dealings of God with his soul: 'I, like a fool, summoned my Husband and Lord, and libelled unkindness against Him; but now I pass from that foolish pursuit.'[11] It is in this letter that he pens the well-known words, hammered from the furnace of suffering: 'I see grace groweth best in winter.'[12]

Lady Culross herself had known the sharp blast of winter in her personal circumstances. Her marriage to James, second Lord Colvill of Culross, brought little consolation, for he did not share her spiritual convictions. Her sons too grew up in unbelief and one, Samuel Colvill, wrote later ridiculing the sufferings of the Covenanters. These things lay as a heavy burden on Lady Culross, and writing to John Livingstone, she shares her concern, 'Guiltiness in me and mine is my greatest cross . . . I would if it were the Lord's will, choose affliction rather than sin.'[13]

Writing to console Lady Culross in these circumstances, Rutherford says: 'As for your son, who is your grief, your

Lord waited on you and me, till we were ripe, and brought us in. It is your part to pray and wait upon Him.'[14] But in the same letter he reminds her, lest she should be too discouraged, of the faithful stand taken by one of her daughters for the truth's sake.

During his twenty-two months of exile in Aberdeen, Rutherford's spirit sometimes soared to the heights and he seemed ushered to the borders of heaven itself, but then he could be plunged into self-condemnation and gloom. To few could he commit these changeable experiences and it is a tribute to the quality of Lady Culross' own spiritual life that she was numbered among this select group. 'My ebbings are very low, and the tide is far out when my Beloved goeth away; and then I cry, "Oh, cruelty! to put out the poor man's one eye,"' Rutherford complained. Then a moment later he exclaims, 'Surely I have not expressed all His sweet kindness to me. I spare to do it, lest I be deemed to seek myself . . . I verily judge that we know not how much may be had in this life.'[15] Little wonder that he could say to Lady Culross, 'I know not whether joy or heaviness in my soul carrieth it away.'[16]

While Rutherford was exiled in Aberdeen, many Christian men and women were also facing increasing opposition from the bishops. John Livingstone, together with Robert Blair and others who had preached in Ireland, experienced continual harassment from the Bishop of Down. At last Livingstone decided to join that intrepid group of men and women who attempted to emigrate to New England in 1636. There they hoped to establish the worship of God in accordance with the dictates of conscience. But as we have seen, adverse weather brought the expedition to near disaster, compelling a return to the homeland. However, God's overruling providence could clearly be traced, for in 1638 Livingstone was at last able to conduct his ministry unmolested, first at Stranraer for ten years and then for fourteen years at Ancrum in the Scottish Borders near the scenes of Rutherford's boyhood days.

This abortive journey to the New World provided the occasion for the only letter preserved to us that Rutherford wrote to John Livingstone. Doubtless there were others, for these two had already been associates for long years in the cause of the gospel. Rutherford had been exiled in Aberdeen just four months at the time and hard months they had proved. Overwhelmed by a sense of isolation, he longed for letters from his friends: 'I bear your name to Christ's door; I pray you, dear brother, forget me not. Let me hear from you by a letter,' he pleads. Rutherford felt deeply for Livingstone's disappointment: 'I suffer with you in grief, for the dash that your desires to be at New England have received of late; but if our Lord, who hath skill to bring up His children, had not seen it your best, it would not have befallen you,'[17] he assures his friend.

With accurate spiritual insight, Rutherford shares his forebodings for the Church of Jesus Christ in Scotland. 'The night is fallen down upon the prophets! Scotland's day of visitation is come.' Rutherford lived long enough to see the Covenants that bound the Scottish Church to Reformation truths trampled under foot at the Restoration of Charles II and the cause for which he and John Livingstone had laboured all but lost. He did not live to see the fulfilment of the second part of his prediction: 'But our sky will clear again; the dry branch of cut-down Lebanon will bud again and be glorious, and they shall yet plant vines upon our mountains.'[18]

In the controversy of the Resolutioners and Protesters, Livingstone espoused the Protesters' cause, but like Robert Blair, his heart was heavy at the dissension that 'hid the godly from the godly'. In a letter to Blair, he laments the situation: 'Blindness and bitterness is the plague of this time . . . my poor wife and I have had more bitterness in that respect now these several months, than ever we had since we could discern what bitterness meant.'[19] Unlike subsequent writers on the character of Samuel Rutherford, he was able to overlook the occasional intolerant invective of which his friend could be guilty and could still describe him as 'a most profound and learned man . . . and a most heavenly Christian as was in his time.'[20]

At the Restoration, days of persecution returned and many faithful ministers knew that their liberty would be short-lived. John Livingstone had been involved in negotiations with Charles on behalf of the Church many years earlier and the King was well aware that here was a man deeply dissatisfied with his monarch's way of life. Not many months later, he was summoned to stand trial in Edinburgh for his unwillingness to acknowledge the authority of the King's prelates in church affairs. Livingstone was served with an order of banishment and was even refused permission to see his wife, Janet, and family once more. Early in 1663 he sailed for Rotterdam. Janet and his two younger children followed him but never again was he to see his five older children.

Ten years of life remained for John Livingstone. He took some part in the ministry of the Scottish church in Rotterdam but most of his time was spent in translating the Scriptures. He planned to publish a copy of the Old Testament with the Hebrew on one half of the page and the most accurate Latin version available on the other. Marginal notes were to be added to the text, explaining difficult passages and reconciling apparently contradictory renderings. The labour was fraught with problems and Livingstone saw little fruit for his endeavours.

Long hours of close study undermined Livingstone's health and he was often in pain. Still he toiled on, but the end came on August 9th, 1672. Some of his friends, co-sufferers in the same cause, gathered round his bed and heard his uncompromised dying testimony: 'I die in the faith that the truths of God which He hath helped the Church of Scotland to own, shall be owned by Him as truths so long as sun and moon endure . . . I have not much to do now with creatures . . . and it is like our parting will be but for a short time . . . '21

So John Livingstone joined Samuel Rutherford, Lady Culross and many another servant of Jesus Christ in a land where the exile and stranger may for ever dwell at peace. It was even as Lady Culross had written those many years before: 'The pain is but for a moment, the pleasure everlasting. The battle is but short, your Captain fights for you, therefore the victory is certain and the reward glorious.'22

James Guthrie and William Guthrie:
Dying Honourably

'Ye will have the advantage of me,' said William Guthrie gloomily to his cousin James one day, 'for ye will die honourably before many witnesses with a rope about your neck, but I shall die whining on a pickle [bit of] straw.' Long years were to pass before the prediction was in part fulfilled, but William had already detected in his cousin a single-hearted, undeviating determination to hold fast to the truth, cost what it may. And of such stuff are martyrs made.

It had not always been so. James Guthrie was born in 1614 into a landed and aristocratic family. His father, the Laird of Guthrie, held high hopes for his son James and what better path could he guide him along than the path to the bishop's mitre? Charles I held rigidly to his father's policy of 'no bishop, no king' and in those days the ladder to worldly success was distinctly episcopal.

James went along with his father's plans happily enough, but God willed otherwise. After a grammar school education in which he excelled at the classics, James proceeded to St Andrews University to study philosophy, hoping from there to enter the Church. His views then, as he tells us himself, were 'prelatic and strong for the ceremonies'. In 1637 the religious situation in Scotland had reached crisis point, as we have seen, erupting into popular protest against Archbishop Laud's new prayer book. The National Covenant of 1638 followed hard on these events and much of the community was caught up in religious and national euphoria. James Guthrie was undecided. Religion to him had previously been only the pathway to advancement, but now new thoughts filled his mind. The world was at his feet academically, for at twenty-three years of age he had already become a professor of philosophy at St Andrews. Yet God was wrestling with the young man and the challenge of the National Covenant brought issues to a head.

Apprehensively, James Guthrie joined the throngs merging on Greyfriar's Churchyard in February 1638. He would add his name to this historic document, setting forth a nation's charter for purity of doctrine and freedom of conscience in worship. But he was nearly deterred. Unexpectedly, he crossed the path of the public hangman and to his troubled mind this was a portent of things to come. Dismayed, the young man paced up and down in an anguish of indecision. Then in a swift moment of resolution, he stepped forward and signed the Covenant. From hence his course led inexorably onwards till it ended in his own martyr's death in 1661.

In 1639 Samuel Rutherford became Professor of Divinity at St Mary's College in St Andrews. It was the beginning of a lifelong association which was to have a profound influence on James Guthrie. Many were the hours the two men spent locked together in conversation as they hammered out the issues that still perplexed Guthrie. Rutherford was in every way fitted to influence him. His philosophical cast of mind and his theological attainments gained Guthrie's respect. But his spirituality and devotion to Christ spoke more strongly than any force of argument. At a weekly gathering for conference and prayer Guthrie met other men of like mind and many bonds of friendship were forged.

*   *   *

William Guthrie was six years younger than his cousin. Also born into an aristocratic family, William had early advantages for he had little to unlearn and his parents witnessed four out of their five sons devote their energies to the gospel ministry. When William arrived at St Andrews to study, his cousin James was already there and he took his young relative under his care, sharing accommodation and instructing him in the truth. One privilege followed on another for William Guthrie. After completing his degree, he proceeded to St Mary's College, there to study divinity under Samuel Rutherford. It was as a direct result of this association with Rutherford that William was converted and called to the ministry. 'There and then,' writes Robert Trail of the young Guthrie, 'it pleased the Lord . . . to call him by his grace by the ministry of the excellent Mr. Samuel Rutherford; and this young man became one of the first-fruits of his ministry at St Andrews.'[1] This marked the transition for William Guthrie from formal to inward heart religion and it was followed swiftly by a secret work of God separating him for the ministry.

Shortly the cousins were to part: James to Lauder first and then, in 1650, to Stirling. William, meanwhile, after preliminary difficulties, settled at Fenwick, near Kilmarnock. Both exercised powerful ministries but the stamp of Samuel Rutherford was indelibly branded upon them. Like Rutherford, William Guthrie had an ardent love for his country charge and no offer of bigger and better opportunities could induce him to leave. With Rutherford, he could say to his Fenwick congregation, 'My only joy, out of heaven, is to hear that the seed of God sown among you is growing and coming to a harvest.'[2] He strove ceaselessly and by all means to win these rural people for the Son of God.

Many were the difficulties William Guthrie faced in his early days at Fenwick, for the prejudice of the people against religion of any sort seemed insurmountable. But not to

William Guthrie. Stories of his ingenuity in winning a hearing for the gospel led to many a raised eyebrow even in his own day. But God owned his ministry, the church eventually becoming so crowded that many had to stand at open windows to hear the preacher's voice. A contemporary record has suggested that thousands were converted to Christ.

One well-meaning hearer contrived, by means unknown, to secure some of William Guthrie's sermon notes on Isaiah 55. These he strung together and published anonymously under the pretentious title *A clear, attractive warming Beam of Light, from Christ, the Sun of Light, leading unto himself.* Guthrie was dismayed! Though 'confusedly huddled together by an injudicious hand',[3] it was recognizable as the preaching of the Fenwick pastor and he had no option but to publish an accurate version of his sermons. So it was that the little volume *The Christian's Great Interest* was born: a work so used of God that the great and humble Dr John Owen declared that it contained more divinity than all the weighty folios he himself had written.

William Guthrie was truly Samuel Rutherford's son in the faith. Bereaved of all his own sons, Rutherford followed Guthrie's career with deep interest and rejoiced at the blessings attending his preaching. On several occasions Guthrie was commissioned by the General Assembly to act as chaplain in the Scottish army both during the First Civil War and more especially at the Battle of Dunbar. This was the occasion when the Scottish troops were routed by the English army on September 3rd, 1650. The only letter from Rutherford to Guthrie which has survived was written against this background. A rumour had reached St Andrews that in the wake of this defeat, Guthrie and others highly esteemed by Rutherford were being forced into a position of compromise and were collaborating with avowed enemies of the Covenants in order to establish Charles as King. The rumour was false, but Rutherford was alarmed and wrote in haste, 'You are much suspected of intended compliance; I mean, not of you only, but of all the people of God with you.'[4] But Rutherford's knowledge of William Guthrie forbade him to entertain the suspicion seriously; yet lest his friend should waver, Rutherford plies him with reasons to forestall any weakening of his position. His own sufferings form a most persuasive entreaty: 'I have suffered much; but this is the thickest darkness, and the straightest step of the way I have yet trodden.' But such an argument must fade before an all compelling spiritual plea: 'Let me obtest [call as witness] all the serious seekers of His face, His secret sealed ones, by the strongest consolations of the Spirit . . . by your last accounts and appearing before God . . . be not deceived by their fair words.'[5]

Not only did Guthrie stand clear of any ungodly liaison but, with his cousin, James, he was one of the men behind the 'Western Remonstrance', a document drawn up by some of the army officers in the west condemning the treaty made with Charles and the attempt to force England to accept him as King. It was a document Charles II never forgot or forgave and vengeance was stored up in his heart for all who had any part in it. Never had Guthrie held a sanguine view of his sovereign. His gloomy foreboding was voiced in a public prayer at the Restoration in 1660: 'Lord, thou knowest how soon this man may welter in the best blood of Scotland.' This was to be tragically fulfilled.

* * *

Throughout the period 1640–1660 James Guthrie had also laboured faithfully in the ministry. Writing to him from London in 1646, Rutherford shares his misgivings and fears concerning the religious situation both in Scotland and in England – 'It is not, I fear, so near to the dawning of the day of salvation but the clouds must send down more showers of blood to water the vineyard of the Lord, and to cause it to blossom! Scotland's scum is not yet removed; nor is England's dross and tin taken away.'[6] Rutherford was clearly much discouraged when he wrote those words and as once he was used of God to enlighten James Guthrie, so now he solicits his prayers. 'I am at low ebb, as to any sensible [conscious] communion with Christ;' he confesses, 'yea, as low as any soul can be, and do scarce know where I am'.[7] Rarely was Rutherford so cast down, but even as he complains of the condition, he supplies the cure: 'The more of the disease there is, the more of the physician's art of grace and tenderness there must be . . . Millions of hells of sinners cannot come near to exhaust infinite grace.'[8]

James Guthrie was fearless in his advocacy of the truth. In 1651 he actually preached against the Public Resolutions which, censuring as he did the chief nobles surrounding their newly-crowned King, was tantamount to a verbal attack on the King himself. He was summoned to Perth to give an account of himself and appears to have come off the better, at least temporarily, on this occasion. In 1659 it fell to this intrepid preacher to pronounce, on behalf of the General Assembly, an excommunication on the Earl of Middleton, for the part the Earl had played in an intrigue with Charles. It was a fearsome undertaking, but Guthrie was not the man to turn aside once he knew his duty. This was the longest nail yet in his coffin.

Well did Oliver Cromwell call James Guthrie 'the short man who could not bow'. Once convicted of the rightness of a cause, neither king nor potentate, persuasion or fear could entice him to deviate. But James Guthrie was not a contentious man. John Howie tells us that he shone above his contemporaries for his peaceable disposition. If tempers became frayed over some matter under discussion, he would often say, 'Enough of this, let us go on to some other subject;

we are warm and can dispute no longer with advantage.'[9] Howie continues by asserting, 'Perhaps he had the greatest mixture of fervent zeal and sweet calmness in his temper of any man in his time.' Though an ardent Protester, James Guthrie took little delight in the sad divisions that set spiritual men at variance one with another. But many who subscribed to the Resolutioners' position did not show an equal degree of charity. Numerous were the calumnies heaped on the head of this good man, particularly after he had written several pamphlets setting out his convictions.

*　　*　　*

We can scarcely be surprised that the first name on Charles II's black list when he was restored to his kingdom and power in 1660 was James Guthrie. He was too outspoken to live and the Earl of Middleton, too, had some old scores to settle. Shortly after the King's return, twelve men met to compose a message of congratulation, pledging their allegiance but also humbly reminding the King of his vows of loyalty to the Covenants. James Guthrie was one of these men. This was pretext enough for the embittered monarch, whose vocabulary contained no word for 'gratitude'. The men were rudely interrupted in their exercise, their papers confiscated and they themselves thrust into ward in Edinburgh Castle. Never again was James Guthrie to be free.

Samuel Rutherford, now clearly dying, was a sad spectator of these events. He wrote a letter of encouragement to the twelve sufferers, so aligning himself with their views and putting himself at great risk. 'Fear not ye. Ye are not, ye shall not be, alone: the Father is with you.' Rutherford knew well that his own name was on Charles II's short list, but his desire to please his God was his master passion: 'If Christ doth own me, let me be in the grave in a bloody winding sheet, and go from the scaffold in four quarters, to grave or no grave.'[10] Such words were written to embolden Guthrie and his friends in their hour of testing. In the event Guthrie was brought to trial after some months of imprisonment, first at Stirling, then Dundee and then back in Edinburgh.

'My conscience I cannot submit.' These words spoken at Guthrie's last defence in April 1661 hold the secret of his triumph in his last extremity, for they were the key to a lifetime of obedience to a will higher than his own. 'But this crazy old body [and he was only forty-seven years of age] and mortal flesh I do submit to do with it whatsoever ye will, whether by death, or banishment or imprisonment or anything else.'[11] The indictment was a flimsy disguise for the hatred and prejudice long stored up against James Guthrie. Engineered by the revengeful Earl of Middleton, the charge accused him of having part in the Western Remonstrance, with injudicious preaching against the Public Resolutions and with a pamphlet he had written entitled *The Causes of the Lord's Wrath against Scotland*. For these offences this good man must die.

Samuel Rutherford was spared the knowledge of the martyrdom of his friend, for just two months earlier his own death put him beyond the reach of wicked men. But he too was fully prepared to pay the ultimate price and said as he was dying, 'Now my tabernacle is weak and I would think it a more glorious way of going home to lay down my life for this cause at the Cross of Edinburgh or St Andrews; but I submit to my Master's will.'[12] James Guthrie shared this view. He once declared that he regarded a martyr's death the most desirable road from time to eternity. In full possession of every faculty, with heightened faith and hope a man might step from the scaffold straight into the arms of his Redeemer; and could there be a better way to die?

Only weeks before his death, Samuel Rutherford wrote one last letter to his friend, Guthrie. It is a letter from one sufferer to another. When Christians die it is common for the foundation truths of the faith to shine out most clearly and in this letter Rutherford could rejoice in the covering of all his life's sins. And the cause for which these men suffered was paramount in his mind: the secular power of the day was usurping authority over 'the royal crown, and absolute supremacy of our Lord Jesus Christ, the Prince of the kings of the earth'.[13] To prevent this, these two, and many others with them, were ready to die.

Rutherford, though not living to see the end, had little doubt of how events would fall out. 'The kingdom of heaven consisteth in a fair company of glorified martyrs and witnesses; of whom Jesus Christ is the chief witness,' he wrote in this last letter. But he was not unmindful of Guthrie's wife and the two little children, Sophia and Willie, so soon to be left alone. 'Cast the burden of wife and children on the Lord Christ,' he advises. 'He careth for you and them. Your blood is precious in His sight.'[14]

On June 1, 1661, James Guthrie was led out to the Grassmarket, the place of execution. Calmly and fearlessly he went and his last speech to the vast concourse of men and women who waited with numb incredulity was long to be remembered. In words both lucid and uncompromised he spoke from the foot of the scaffold: 'I take God to record upon my soul, I would not exchange this scaffold with the palace or mitre of the greatest prelate in Britain.' Then mounting the ladder a few rungs his scaffold became his last pulpit as he held forth Christ to the people: 'Jesus Christ is my light and my life, my righteousness, my strength and my salvation and all my desire. Him! Him! I do with all the strength of my soul commend to you.' Lifting the cloth that covered his eyes moments before he suffered, he called out 'The Covenants, the Covenants shall yet be Scotland's reviving.' And so he died. To fill the cup of wrath to its brim, they severed his head from his body and for twenty-seven long years it remained high up on the Netherbow bleached by sun and wind: a testimony of condemnation against a godless regime.

*   *   *

As William Guthrie had predicted, so James had died: honourably, with a rope about his neck and before many witnesses. William earnestly wished to attend his cousin at the scaffold, caring for him till the last, but the days were corrupt and the entreaties of his parishioners prevailed on William to avoid so great a risk for his life too had a price tag on it.

All his days William Guthrie had suffered ill health but by his cheerful disposition and sensible precautions he had generally maintained physical well-being. But his cousin's cruel death struck a severe blow. Three years later his own ministry was taken from him by the Archbishop of Glasgow. No one could be found willing to perform the prelate's dastardly deed and evict so highly respected a man. At last some miserable curate was hired to go to Fenwick and declare that William Guthrie must quit both pulpit and manse. Receiving early warning of the event, Guthrie had already preached his customary two sermons to his distressed people before nine o'clock in the morning. When the Archbishop's emissary arrived, the people were dispersing. Calling first at the manse to deliver his unwelcome message, he proceeded to the church. Finding it empty, he preached in Guthrie's pulpit himself to a handful of his own soldier-band.

The silenced pastor continued living in Fenwick for the time being, but his health soon broke completely though he was only forty-five years of age. The end was hard, very hard. The violent pains he suffered were so intense that his friends were obliged to hold him down. But he did not 'die whining on a pickle straw'. The truth was that he died a hero. Between the attacks of pain he was able to murmur, 'Though I should die mad, yet I know I shall die in the Lord.' Even in his extremity he judged his Lord to be good to a sinner such as he. He longed for the moment of his release but patiently waited God's time to call him away from the sorrows of earth. After eight or ten days of acute suffering, God granted his desire and, like his cousin James, William Guthrie too died honourably.

14

Robert M'Ward:
Christ's Exile

A simple ordination service was in progress in Rotterdam in the year 1679. Three men rose to lay hands on the head of a young preacher, commissioning him in the name of the Lord Jesus to the solemn task of proclaiming the gospel to his fellow-men. But this young man received not only an ordination to preach, but an ordination to suffer. Two lifted their hands, but one, an old man, still stood by the kneeling figure, his hands resting on the bowed head. Suddenly he declared, 'Behold, all ye spectators. Here is the head of a faithful minister and servant of Jesus Christ, who shall lose the same for his Master's interest; and it shall be set up before the sun and the moon in the public view of the world.'[1]

Such was the ordination of young Richard Cameron. Only one crowded, colourful year was to run before the old man's prediction was fulfilled: a year of preaching, praying, escaping and resisting as Cameron became the acknowledged leader of the dispirited Covenanter remnant. It was at Ayrsmoss in July 1680 that the 'Lion of the Covenant' (a name given to him long years after) was at last hunted down. He and his men put up a valiant fight against impossible odds, but calling out, 'Lord, spare the green and take the ripe,' Richard Cameron was killed and his brother, Michael, with him. His head was severed from his body and kicked around like a football before being fixed high on the Netherbow, an intended object lesson for all who passed by.

The old man who so accurately predicted Cameron's death was Robert M'Ward, lifelong friend of Samuel Rutherford and exile from his native shores for twenty long years. How could he have uttered such words? Long communion with God, coupled with his own baptism of suffering, had taught Robert M'Ward and his fellow exiles much of the ways of God and also the vile depths to which unregenerate man could stoop. Many were the prophetic utterances recorded from those days and some, like this one, were fulfilled with remarkable accuracy. Asked of the truth of his prediction after Cameron's death, M'Ward replied, 'Indeed, 'tis most true; and it was no foresight or forethoughts in me, but when my hand was upon his head, I was as much persuaded of it . . . as if I had been at Ayrsmoss.'[2]

As a young man, Robert M'Ward studied his divinity at St Andrews, sitting under the instruction of Samuel Rutherford. A peculiar bond of affection sprang up between master and pupil and it was M'Ward who was honoured to travel to London in 1643 to act as amanuensis for Rutherford at the Westminster Assembly. For four years they worked closely together, M'Ward's admiration and respect undiminishing, despite having to learn, with Rutherford, much needed lessons in mutual toleration of fellow-believers and continual self-denial to the accomplishing of a great end.

About the year 1655, Robert M'Ward was ordained to the ministry and in 1656 he succeeded Andrew Gray at the Outer High Church in Glasgow. This was no easy task, for Andrew Gray was a young man of rare talent and godliness who had entered the ministry at the early age of twenty. For twenty-two months the crowds flocked to hear him preach and John Howie tells us that his style was 'very warm and rapturous, and well adapted to affect the hearts of his hearers.' Gray had a premonition, however, that he would not live beyond his twenty-second year, and he was right. Though his course was quickly run, his usefulness had been remarkable for one so young. Howie assures us: 'He was in his day a most singular and pious youth; and though he died young, he was old in grace, having lived long and done much for God in a little time.'[3] To follow such a man was an unenviable assignment, but Robert M'Ward rose to the challenge and was equally beloved of his people.

For five years he ministered in Glasgow, but his fearless outspoken preaching did not pass unnoticed by the enemies of the Covenant. In 1660 came the year of accounting as Charles 11 was established on the throne. 'Pray for Christ. Preach for Christ . . . Do all for Christ, beware of men-pleasing . . . The Chief Shepherd will shortly appear.'[4] So spoke M'Ward's old tutor, who was on his death-bed at the time, knowing full well that such counsel would lead to inevitable confrontation. M'Ward did just that. In February of that year he preached a week-day sermon, one of a series, in Tron Church, Glasgow; a sermon that called the nation to heart-searching and repentance from the text, 'You only have I known of all the families of the earth: therefore I will punish you for all your inquities.'[5] At that very time the 'Drunken Parliament' was in session and, dominated by the renegade Earl of Middleton, it was undoing at a crazy speed all the work of the Covenants that upheld Reformation principles.

Robert M'Ward ended the series with these heroic words: 'As for my part, as a poor member of the Church of Scotland, and an unworthy minister in it, I do this day call you who are the people of God to witness that I humbly offer my dissent to all Acts which are or shall be passed against the Covenants and work of Reformation in Scotland.'[6] His fate was sealed. This was too much for a government at that very moment bent on condemning the good James Guthrie to death for no greater offence. M'Ward was arrested and brought under guard to Edinburgh. Perhaps the two men shared a common prison and strengthened each other in the face of impending death. Perhaps they shared together words written by Rutherford to Guthrie only six weeks before the former died. We do not know, but the words were equally applicable to both: 'Think it not strange that men devise against you; whether it be to exile, the earth is the Lord's; or perpetual imprisonment, the Lord is your light and liberty; or a violent and public death, for the kingdom of heaven consisteth in a fair company of glorified martyrs and witnesses.'[7]

Robert M'Ward expected to die. From his prison he wrote to Lady Ardross, daughter of Lady Boyd, words that reveal his fears and his faith at this time: 'I hope, Madam . . . that ye will not forget to deal with God in my behalf that now, when it comes to the swellings of Jordan, I may not sink or succumb and desert a cause upon which I am obliged not only to venture my life but some way my soul also which is by sealing that poor testimony with my blood, if he call me to it.'[8]

Robert M'Ward stood trial only five days after the City of Edinburgh had reeled with horror at the shock of Guthrie's execution by the hands of the public hangman and shuddered at the sight of his beloved head high up on the Netherbow between High Street and Canongate. Guthrie's sufferings were engraved indelibly on M'Ward's mind and from those momentous days was born the insight that prompted his declaration that Richard Cameron likewise should be dishonoured of men but honoured of God.

M'Ward did not flinch from paying the ultimate price for his allegiance to Christ, but God willed otherwise. A month of suspense followed the trial and on July 5 an order of banishment for life was served on this faithful minister of Jesus Christ. Shortly after these events M'Ward and his family set sail from Scottish shores for Rotterdam, never to return save for one brief clandestine visit in 1669. There on foreign soil he was to labour in the cause of Christ for the remainder of his life and there he was to die after twenty years of exile.

His companion in exile was John Brown of Wamphray, the son of Jean Brown, Rutherford's friend and correspondent, who had been arrested in September 1662 and held in the Edinburgh Tolbooth. Not content with incarcerating this noble Christian, the Council imposed conditions which brought Brown to the gates of death. Deprived of the essentials of life, his health broke and in this state he was forced to sign a bond of voluntary banishment before he was allowed any improvement in his lot. This is how the enemies of the Covenant treated a man who John Howie tells us was 'famous in his day for learning, faithfulness, warm zeal and true piety'.[9]

So John Brown joined Robert M'Ward in Rotterdam not long after John Livingstone had also arrived. By the spring of 1663 over four hundred Scottish ministers had been evicted from their churches, many to wander homeless from place to place, many to banishment on the Continent. This was in the wake of legislation passed by the Privy Council on October 1, 1662, requiring all ministers installed in churches since 1649 to regularize their position by applying to the bishops. The compromise entailed in such a step was too much for the consciences of most good men and they chose poverty, banishment and silence in loyalty to their Christian principles. Two thousand of England's best men had faced similar sorrows on Black Bartholomew's Day, August 24, 1662. Truly the bride of Christ was clothed in sackcloth.

Although Robert M'Ward might be banished, his usefulness in Christ's service was by no means at an end and he was soon closely associated with the Scottish church in Rotterdam, becoming joint-minister for a brief period. Most of the congregation consisted of exiles who had fled there to escape the fury of persecution; their spiritual needs were great and none was better fitted to minister to them than Robert M'Ward. Like Joseph of old, he was sent ahead of his brethren to make provision for them. Nor did he forget the desperate needs of those remaining in Scotland, hounded to and fro like animals by the remorseless lash of religious intolerance. Some were tempted to compromise, others to take zeal to an extreme and invite reprisals. A steady stream of literature flowed from his ready pen to hearten and sustain his brethren. *The Poor Man's Cup of Cold Water, Ministered to the Saints and Sufferers for Christ in Scotland* was one such title, published in 1679 when persecution rose to a new height following the disastrous defeat of the Covenanters at Bothwell Bridge.

The continual arrival of new exiles kept M'Ward and Brown in close touch with every issue that affected the struggle in the homeland. Each was debated and followed with avid concern, and, like the Apostle Paul, M'Ward could say, 'Who is weak and I am not weak? Who is offended and I burn not?' (*2 Cor. 11.29*). No question was watched more closely by the Rotterdam exiles than that of the Indulgences. Of all the devices of the government to overthrow the Covenanting cause, this apparently conciliatory gesture did more to divide and destroy than the cruellest thrust made by force of arms. Under the First Indulgence of 1669 the persecuted preachers were offered the right to resume their ministry, but the terms, though dressed up to look attractive, were very little different from those which these same men had originally rejected for conscience sake. Forty-two succumbed. Covenanters they might well remain in private, but the terms under which they returned expressly repudiated loyalty to the Covenants of 1638 and 1643. The Second Indulgence, three years later, divided their ranks still further, but even worse than this was the subsequent division of those remaining outside the terms of the Indulgences. Some, while not yielding themselves, took a lenient attitude towards those who had done so. Others felt betrayed by their brethren and severed all links with the Indulged men. Still others refused to retain fellowship, either with those returning to their churches or yet with those who refused to condemn them. It was a controversy that led directly to the defeat of Bothwell Bridge and many a man was more wounded in the house of his friends than by his enemies. The division bore a marked resemblance to the bitter dissension between the Resolutioners and the Protesters of the 1650s and M'Ward, Donald Cargill and John Brown, who had all learnt their theology and principles from the lips of Rutherford, took the stricter line, though it has to be said that a considerable degree of legalism and excess coloured the attitudes of some who held such a position. It was young Richard Cameron's stand on these issues that won for him the support and favour of both M'Ward and Brown, and many a letter of encouragement and advice followed him in his dramatic and short-lived course.

But, like Rutherford before him, it was not in controversy that M'Ward was to make his most lasting contribution to the history of the Christian Church. As Rutherford's outstanding service was his letters, so M'Ward's privilege was to collect them together and then to publish them in 1664.

Attempts had been made during Rutherford's lifetime to make such a collection. An early historian, John Row, himself one of Rutherford's correspondents, writing at least eighteen years before Rutherford's death, says in his *History of the Kirk of Scotland*, 'Sundry began to gather them [the letters] together and have whole books full of them which if they were printed, I am confident through the Lord's rich mercy and blessing would not fail to do much good for in them there are handled many necessary cases of conscience wherein perplexed souls might get resolution.'[10] Although some of the letters had already been circulating in manuscript form for many years, Rutherford adamantly refused to countenance publication. His main reason was a spiritual one: lest any should elevate and overvalue mere man. He was deeply conscious of the corruptions and frailties latent even in the heart of the believer and truly feared the unwarranted praise of men. To Lady Boyd he confesses, 'My white side cometh out on paper to men; but at home and within I find much black work, and great cause of a low sail, and of little boasting.'[11]

So it was that in 1662 the exiled M'Ward, still grieving over the loss of his friend, sent notification all over Scotland of the proposed publication. And so the correspondence, worn and creased with constant rereading, was gathered together in the interests of the greater good of Christ's kingdom. Some contributed their collection of manuscript copies taken from the originals. The title page of the first edition of *Joshua Redivivus or Mr Rutherford's Letters* bears no indication of the place of publication, for these were suffering times and M'Ward himself hid under the anonymity of the words 'By a Wellwisher to the Work and People of God'. But his name was whispered around and many a grateful Covenanter saved up his scant resources to purchase the volume. Rutherford was indeed 'Joshua Redivivus', a second Joshua returned to life again and sent as God's spy into the land of persecution, from there sending messages to stimulate and console his hard-pressed fellow Christians.

M'Ward himself could see a providence of God in the timing of the publication and in Rutherford's refusals during his lifetime. With many preachers ejected from their pulpits and numerous congregations now deprived of the Word of God, M'Ward could write, 'God hath reserved the publication thereof for such a time as this . . . [that] they may in their sad hours commune with this sufferer who speaks to them good words and comfortable. He telleth you, beloved sufferers, what a heaven is to be had in Christ's company even when you are put to bear the cross and to have shame and suffering for His sake.'[12]

Before the period of intense persecution had died down, *Joshua Redivivus; or Mr Rutherford's Letters* had passed through three editions. The third edition, published in 1675, added a further sixty-eight letters to the collection. Robert M'Ward ought to be remembered with gratitude by Christians for the vision and diligence he displayed in this service to the Church of Jesus Christ.

Like Rutherford before him, M'Ward was himself a prolific letter-writer. Letters from this exiled Christian constantly crossed the North Sea to encourage and nerve his fellow-believers. Lady Kenmure was one of his most regular correspondents; their common esteem for Samuel Rutherford naturally drew them together and M'Ward partook much of his master's spirit. Rutherford had died shortly before Lady Kenmure's brother, Archibald, the Marquis of Argyll, was executed in May 1661. These were days, as Archibald expressed it, when a man must either sin or suffer. There was no middle course and the Marquis chose to suffer. M'Ward took it upon himself to fulfil a pastor's role to Lady Kenmure. Having spoken sympathetically of her sufferings and grief, he urges her to look to the greater distress of Christ's Church. 'This calls your ladyship some way to forget the decay and . . . disgrace, of your ever honourable family and father's house, but now more honourable than ever, that ye may remember to weep with Zion and lament because the glory is departed. O the sad days that your ladyship is like to see if He do not shut your eyes in death and receive you in amongst the company of them who have come out of great tribulation and can weep no more because they see God.'[13]

Just fifteen months later, Lady Kenmure saw the dark spectre of the past repeating itself in the experience of her nephew, Archibald's son. Grieved and angry at the treatment his father had received, young Lord Lorn (soon to become the Earl of Argyll) had written a letter expressing his dismay to a friend. The letter was intercepted and became the basis of a charge of treason brought against the young man. In August 1662 he too was sentenced to be beheaded. These were days when there was no justice in the land. Again M'Ward picked up his pen to minister consolation to Lady Kenmure. Again he knew that the truest comfort he could offer was to show her that all these sorrows were but a part of the anguish of the true Church of Christ. ' . . . But, madam, I know, since God has learned you to prefer Jerusalem above your chief joy . . . that ye forget to sorrow for your father's house, and weep when ye remember Zion.'[14] In the event Lady Kenmure was spared from facing so appalling a grief at that time, for after the Earl of Middleton's fall from favour in 1663, Lord Lorn was released.

By 1681 Robert M'Ward was a lonely figure. His life had spanned a long and tumultuous period. How high had been his hopes when he and Donald Cargill had studied together at St Andrews under Rutherford. The days were alive with possibilities under the good hand of God. Four years of life had been devoted to work on the Westminster Confession of Faith as Rutherford's secretary. But he had lived to see all apparently crumble before his eyes. Rutherford had died twenty years previously; Lady Kenmure, frail but courageous to the last, had died in 1672; and in that same year his fellow exile, John Livingstone, had also died. John Brown, his colleague and friend, had ended his pilgrimage in September 1679, while the bitter divisions amongst the Covenanters over the Indulgences nearly broke M'Ward's own health. 'I was so confounded with these cause-destroying excesses that I was thereby, as I suppose you have heard, brought to the gates of death,' he wrote in a letter about this time.[15] Then in July 1680, Richard Cameron was cruelly slaughtered, leaving the 'hill-men' leaderless. It was a dismal picture and only a man with unwavering faith could penetrate the gloom and declare with Samuel Rutherford, 'The bride will yet sing, as in the days of her youth. The dry olive-tree shall bud again, and dry dead bones shall live.'[16] But such a man was Robert M'Ward and when he died on May 26, 1681, the soldier-poet William Cleland could write of him:

> For truth a champion both by tongue and pen,
> Regardless of the wrath and rage of men.
> What pen can write or what tongue can express
> His choicest parts, his worth, his usefulness?[17]

Conclusion:
Rutherford Lives On

> What tongue, what pen or skill of men
> Can famous Rutherford commend?
> His learning justly raised his fame,
> True goodness did adorn his name.

So run the opening lines of the epitaph etched on the old grey tombstone marking the spot where Samuel Rutherford was buried in St Andrew's Cathedral grounds. But when Rutherford died, his most important contribution to the Church of Jesus Christ had scarcely begun. His letters, mainly written during his twenty-two-month period of exile, form his true memorial – letters for which he had resolutely refused publication.

Side by side with Rutherford's headstone stands another commemorating the life of Thomas Halyburton, also a professor of divinity at St Andrews, but living half a century later. Like Rutherford, Halyburton left a heritage of blessing for the people of God in the way he died. Many of the words spoken on his death-bed in 1712 at the age of thirty-eight provide clear evidence that Halyburton had long feasted his mind on the *Letters of Samuel Rutherford*. It was his dying request that he should be buried beside his well-known predecessor. 'I was just thinking', he confessed on the last day of his life, 'of the pleasant plot of earth that I will get to lie in beside Mr Rutherford . . . and O! we will be a knot of bonnie dust.'[1]

Halyburton was only one of a long succession of men and women, many notable in their own right, who have gladly owned a debt of gratitude to the writings of Samuel Rutherford. Their tributes can be traced in an unbroken line, starting from Rutherford's own generation and continuing to the present day. John Brown of Haddington, preacher and theologian, who produced the famous Self-Interpreting Bible in 1778, was once an orphaned shepherd boy. The twelve-year-old child might have been found on the quiet hillside above Abernethy caring for his sheep, engrossed in the *Letters of Samuel Rutherford*. He readily acknowledged the formative influence of this book on his thinking and recommended it warmly to his own children when he was dying.

John Wesley, man of tireless genius, discovered the *Letters* possibly on a visit to Scotland and republished extracts in 1753 as part of *Volume 28* of his *Christian Library*. 'These letters', commented Wesley in a preface to a reprint of his extracts in 1767, 'have been generally admired by all the children of God for the vein of piety, trust in God and holy zeal which runs through them.'[2]

When young Richard Cecil first heard George Whitefield preach in 1766, his conscience was awakened, but he remained unconverted until he saw enacted at his mother's death-bed a sermon without words that profoundly affected and humbled him. Cecil became one of the most influential preachers of the late eighteenth century. His biographer, Josiah Pratt, records Cecil's comments on many of the books then in circulation. For most he has a mixture of praise and complaint but for the *Letters of Samuel Rutherford* he has nothing but appreciation. 'Rutherford's *Letters* is one of my classics. Were truth the beam . . . and all that the world had agreed to idolize weighed against that book, they would be lighter than vanity. He is a real original.'[3]

Although Robert Murray M'Cheyne died at only

twenty-nine years of age, his memory is still held in high regard. His biographer, Andrew Bonar, singles out two books which had a formative influence on M'Cheyne's thinking. One of these was the *Letters of Samuel Rutherford*. From a tribute made at his funeral in 1839, we learn that the letters 'were almost daily his delight'.[4] Andrew Bonar comments on the undeniable influence they had on M'Cheyne: 'The calm, holy, tenderly affectionate style of his letters remind us of Samuel Rutherford whose works he delighted to read.'[5]

Andrew Bonar himself gave many months of his time to preparing a new edition of the *Letters*. Each letter he placed chronologically, prefacing it with a short summary and adding a glossary of difficult words. This edition, first published in 1863, he revised and republished in 1891. It was the eighty-one-year-old Bonar's final editorial labour and has never been bettered. 'I have just finished what may be my last literary work,' he wrote on April 12 of that year; 'got much from it to my own soul all the time. The love of Christ that filled his heart throws out its sparks as we read.'[6]

In a review of this 1891 edition for *The Sword and Trowel* magazine, Charles Haddon Spurgeon, still bearing the scars of the Downgrade Controversy, wrote his often-quoted appraisal: 'There is, to us, something mysterious, awe-creating and superhuman about Rutherford's letters . . . One page is worth a thousand tomes of the Downgrade frothiness.' Spurgeon himself was of kindred spirit with the great Covenanter. They were one in theological persuasion, spiritual warmth and poetic gift. Little wonder that Spurgeon should conclude that review with these words: 'When we are dead and gone let the world know that Spurgeon held Rutherford's *Letters* to be the nearest thing to inspiration which can be found in all the writings of mere men.'[7] It is fitting that the last hymn Spurgeon sang at a simple bedside service as he lay dying in Mentone in January

1892 was Anne Ross Cousin's rendering of many of Rutherford's words:

> The sands of time are sinking,
> The dawn of heaven breaks.
> The summer morn I've sighed for,
> The fair sweet morn awakes.

Bonar's highly popular edition of the *Letters* went through five impressions and the name of Samuel Rutherford became known in some of the farthest corners of the earth. Many a missionary left his homeland with a valued copy packed in his trunk. The writings of James Hudson Taylor, founder of the China Inland Mission, reflect the influence of the old Scottish divine. This is particularly true of his popular *Union and Communion*, a study in the *Song of Songs* published in book form in 1914. He himself often drew consolation from the *Letters* when days were hard and his spirit discouraged.[8] Fred Mitchell, Home Director of that same mission from 1943–1953, wrote to his friend Wilbur Smith telling him that he planned to write a book on Rutherford drawing on material he had collected over the years.[9] His premature death in an air crash cut short these hopes.

Jock Purves, missionary, traveller, preacher and writer, is best remembered for his book *Fair Sunshine*, covering the life and testimony of thirteen Covenanting heroes. One does not have to read far before discovering that the study of the *Letters* was one of Purves' lifelong joys. 'Three hundred and sixty-five letters,' he wrote, 'one a day to read for a year! Never voice spoke out of a heart more abundantly filled with the love of Christ.'[10] Faced with his own last illness in 1988, Jock Purves was still deriving benefit from the *Letters of Samuel Rutherford* and could write: 'And oh! that quotation from S.R. "My faith hath no bed to sleep on but omnipotency", MARVELLOUS! WONDERFUL! I think about it all the time.'

Most of these names are well known. But they are not alone and must surely represent a host of men and women, unknown and unnamed, who will rise up in the last day and thank God for the small fair-haired letter-writer from Anwoth who showed them the loveliness of Christ.

NOTES

CHAPTER I

1. C.H. Spurgeon, *The Sword and Trowel*, June 1891.
2. *Letters of Samuel Rutherford*, Bonar Edition 1891, republished Banner of Truth Trust, 1984, (hereafter referred to as LSR) 344, p. 680.
3. LSR 186, p. 364.
4. LSR 232, pp. 460–1.
5. LSR 222, p. 431.
6. LSR 285, p. 556.
7. LSR 233, p. 261.
8. LSR 225, p. 438.
9. Ibid., p. 439.
10. Patrick Simpson, Wodrow MSS, Quoted by Thomas McCrie, *The Story of the Scottish Church*, Free Presbyterian Productions, 1988, p. 250.
11. LSR 279, pp. 540–1.
12. LSR 5, p. 43.
13. Ibid.
14. Patrick Simpson, op. cit.
15. Robert Wodrow, *The History of the Sufferings of the Church of Scotland*, 1828, vol. 1, p. 205.
16. LSR 14, p. 59.
17. LSR 11, p. 50.
18. LSR 105, p. 217.
19. LSR 187, p. 367.
20. LSR 56, p. 129.
21. *Exercitationes Apologeticae pro Divina Gratia*, 1636.
22. LSR 61, p. 137.
23. LSR 185, p. 362.
24. LSR 97, p. 203.

25. LSR 225, p. 438.
26. LSR 76, p. 162.
27. LSR 182, p. 354.
28. LSR 179, pp. 341–2.
29. LSR 226, p. 446.
30. LSR 36, p. 99.
31. LSR 287, pp. 565–7.
32. LSR 193, p. 380.
33. LSR 84, p. 177.
34. LSR 282, p. 547.
35. LSR 180, p. 347.
36. LSR 300, p. 608.
37. LSR 4, pp. 41–2.
38. Robert Baillie, *The Letters and Journals*, Edinburgh, 1841, vol. 1, p. 79.
39. Quoted by John Gillies, *Historical Collections of Accounts of Revival*, Banner of Truth Trust, 1981, p. 201.
40. LSR 287, p. 567.
41. Robert M'Ward, Preface to *Joshua Redivivus or Mr Rutherford's Letters*, 1664.
42. Preface to *A Survey of the Spiritual Antichrist*, 1648.
43. LSR 310, p. 621.
44. LSR 338, p. 671.
45. LSR 353, p. 686.
46. Wodrow's *Analecta*, MS iv. Quoted by Thomas McCrie, op. cit., p. 250.
47. Thomas McCrie, op. cit., p. 238.
48. Rutherford's *Testimony*, LSR, Thomas Smith Edition, 1881, p. 36.
49. A. Taylor Innes, *Studies in Scottish History*, 1892, pp. 15–16.
50. Alexander Whyte, *Samuel Rutherford and Some of His Correspondents*, 1894, p. 11.
51. Robert Gilmour, *Samuel Rutherford: A Study*, 1904, pp. 22–3.
52. LSR 341, p. 674.
53. LSR 348, p. 683.
54. LSR 354, p. 688.
55. John Macleod, *Scottish Theology*, Edinburgh, 1943, p. 72.
56. John Knox, *The History of the Reformation*, Banner of Truth Trust, 1982, pp. 278–9.
57. From an old record of Rutherford's dying words written shortly after his death and found in several early accounts and also John Howie, *The Scots Worthies*, 1775, p. 201.

58. LSR 22, p. 75.
59. LSR 321, p. 639.
60. LSR 4, p. 42.
61. LSR 84, p. 178.
62. Thomas McCrie, *The Life of John Knox*, Free Presbyterian Publications, 1978, pp. 253–4.
63. LSR 130, p. 256.
64. Robert Gilmour, op. cit., p. 229.
65. Alexander Smellie, *Men of the Covenant*, Banner of Truth Trust, 1960, p. 22.
66. See note 57, John Howie, p. 202.
67. LSR 333, p. 662.
68. See note 57, John Howie, p. 201.
69. A.R. Cousin, *Last Words of Samuel Rutherford*, LSR, p. 744.

CHAPTER 2

1. LSR 22, p. 77.
2. LSR 34, p. 96.
3. LSR 18, p. 66.
4. Samuel Rutherford, *Communion Sermons*, Reprinted J.A. Dickson, 1986, p. 254.
5. Alexander Whyte, *Samuel Rutherford and Some of His Correspondents*, 1894, p. 27.
6. LSR 179, p. 336.
7. LSR 185, pp. 361–2.
8. LSR 8, p. 49.
9. LSR 6, p. 45.
10. Several letters relating to this issue appear to be out of chronological order in Bonar's 1891 edition. Amongst these is Letter 49 which is placed in 1635 but refers to Lord Kenmure as being alive though he died in September 1634.
11. LSR 46, pp. 114–5.
12. LSR 51, p. 123.
13. LSR 14, pp. 59–60.
14. LSR 67, p. 146.
15. LSR 243, p. 481.
16. LSR 221, p. 431.
17. LSR 177, p. 337.
18. LSR 41, p. 107.
19. LSR 80, p. 169.
20. LSR 17, p. 64.
21. LSR 26, p. 85.

22. LSR 221, pp. 430–1.
23. LSR 288, p. 570.
24. LSR 126, p. 250.
25. LSR 177, p. 337.

CHAPTER 3

1. LSR 82, p. 172.
2. LSR 82, p. 171.
3. LSR 82, p. 173.
4. LSR 82, p. 171.
5. LSR 82, pp. 172–3.
6. LSR 180, p. 344.
7. LSR 180, p. 345.
8. Ibid.
9. LSR 180, p. 347.
10. LSR 82, p. 172.
11. LSR 124, p. 249.
12. Ibid.
13. LSR 82, p. 172.
14. LSR 124, p. 249.
15. LSR 100, p. 209.
16. LSR 192, p. 379.
17. LSR 100, p. 209.
18. Ibid.
19. LSR 192, p. 379.
20. LSR 103, p. 214.
21. Ibid.
22. LSR 180, p. 344.
23. LSR 82, p. 171.
24. Ibid.
25. LSR 173, p. 324.
26. LSR 173, p. 326.
27. LSR 173, p. 325.
28. Ibid.
29. Ibid.
30. Ibid.
31. LSR 123, p. 248.
32. Alexander Whyte, *Samuel Rutherford and Some of His Correspondents*, 1894, p. 82.
33. Others have followed Whyte in this interpretation, including the Rev. G.N.M. Collins in his Evangelical Library Annual Lecture of 1961 entitled: *Samuel Rutherford: Saint and Statesman*, p. 13.

34. LSR 123, p. 247.
35. LSR 123, p. 248.
36. Deuteronomy 29:29.
37. Wodrow MSS, vol. 29.
38. LSR 173, p. 324.

CHAPTER 4

1. Bonar's Introduction to LSR 75, p. 158.
2. LSR 130, p. 256.
3. LSR 75, p. 160.
4. LSR 22, p. 75.
5. LSR 22, p. 77.
6. LSR 22, p. 76.
7. LSR 161, p. 299.
8. LSR 189, p. 372.
9. Bonar's Introduction to LSR 161, p. 298.

CHAPTER 5

1. *Memorable Characteristics*, in *Select Biographies*, Wodrow Society, vol. 1, 1845, p. 318.
2. LSR 63, p. 143.
3. *Livingstone's Memoirs*, in *Select Biographies*, Wodrow Society, vol. 1, 1845, p. 305.
4. *Memorable Characteristics*, p. 316.
5. Wodrow's MSS, Advocate's Library, Edinburgh. Quoted by Thomas McCrie, *The Story of the Scottish Church*, Free Presbyterian Publications, 1988, p. 242.
6. Robert Wodrow, *Life of David Dickson*, in *Select Biographies*, Wodrow Society, vol. 2, 1847, p. 9.
7. LSR 110, p. 226.
8. Republished Banner of Truth Trust, 1959, 1978, 1981.
9. A. Bonar, Introduction to LSR, p. 19.
10. LSR 119, p. 241.
11. LSR 168, p. 316.
12. LSR 259, p. 508.
13. LSR 167, p. 314.
14. LSR 168, pp. 315–6.
15. A. Bonar's Introduction to LSR 298, p. 602.
16. LSR 298, p. 602.
17. LSR 168, p. 315.
18. A.B. Grosart, *Representative Non-Conformists*, 1879, p. 202.

19. Wodrow's *Analecta*, MS. Quoted by Thomas McCrie, op. cit., pp. 238–9.
20. *Memorable Characteristics*, p. 319.

CHAPTER 6

1. LSR 89, p. 188.
2. Robert Wodrow, *The Life of Robert Blair*, Wodrow Society, 1848, p. 2.
3. Ibid., p. 5.
4. Psalm 73:28.
5. Robert Wodrow, op. cit., p. 12.
6. Ibid., p. 17.
7. Ibid., p. 96.
8. LSR 63, p. 142.
9. LSR 89, pp. 189–90.
10. Wodrow's MSS, Advocate's Library. Quoted by Thomas McCrie, op. cit., p. 242.
11. Robert Wodrow, op. cit., p. 263.
12. From an early MS quoted by John Howie, *The Scots Worthies*, 1775, p. 201.
13. Ibid.
14. LSR 333, p. 662.

CHAPTER 7

1. LSR 321, p. 639.
2. *Memorable Characteristics*, in *Select Biographies*, Wodrow Society, vol. 1, p. 347.
3. LSR 309, p. 618.
4. Andrew Stevenson, *History of the Church and State of Scotland*, 1840, p. 436.
5. *Memorable Characteristics*, p. 347.
6. James Anderson, *The Ladies of the Covenant*, 1862, p. 17.
7. LSR 107, pp. 220–1.
8. London, 1647.
9. LSR 107, p. 221.
10. LSR 107, p. 220.
11. LSR 294, p. 592.
12. LSR 299, pp. 604–5.
13. LSR 232, pp. 460–2.
14. LSR 321, p. 639.

CHAPTER 8

1. *Memorable Characteristics*, in *Select Biographies*, Wodrow Society, vol. 1, p. 343.
2. Samuel Rutherford, *Quaint Sermons Hitherto Unpublished*, 1885, p. 86.
3. LSR 59, pp. 133–4.
4. Ibid.
5. *Memorable Characteristics*, p. 343.
6. LSR 59, p. 133.
7. LSR 109, p. 223.
8. LSR 323, p. 643.

CHAPTER 9

1. LSR 196, p. 385.
2. LSR 196, p. 384.
3. LSR 196, p. 385.
4. LSR 99, p. 206.
5. LSR 281, p. 526.
6. LSR 99, p. 207.
7. LSR 99, p. 208.
8. LSR 181, p. 350.
9. Ibid.
10. LSR 196, p. 385.
11. John Howie, *The Scots Worthies*, 1775, p. 328.
12. LSR 196, p. 385.
13. LSR 181, p. 352.

CHAPTER 10

1. LSR 144, p. 275.
2. LSR 144, p. 274.
3. Robert Baillie's *Letters*, vol. 1, p. 67.
4. Ibid., p. 419.
5. James Reid, *Memoirs of the Westminster Divines*, Banner of Truth Trust, 1982, p. 282.
6. LSR 324, p. 644.
7. Ibid.
8. Bonar's Introduction to LSR 144, p. 247.
9. Alexander Smellie, *Men of the Covenant*, Banner of Truth Trust, 1960, p. 22.
10. Bonar's Introduction to LSR 144, p. 274.
11. John Howie, *The Scots Worthies*, 1775, p. 170.

12. LSR 324, p. 645.
13. LSR 326, p. 647.

CHAPTER 11

1. Proverbs 31:10.
2. Alexander Smellie, *Men of the Covenant*, Banner of Truth Trust, 1960, p. 175.
3. LSR 131, p. 259.
4. LSR 243, p. 481.
5. LSR 131, p. 258.
6. LSR 84, p. 178.
7. LSR 111, p. 227.
8. Ibid.
9. LSR 131, p. 258.
10. Ibid.
11. LSR 84, p. 177.
12. LSR 84, p. 178.
13. LSR 131, p. 258.
14. Robert Fleming, *Fulfilling of the Scriptures*. Quoted by John Gillies, *Historical Collections of Accounts of Revival*, Banner of Truth Trust, 1981, p. 197.
15. Ibid.
16. Ibid.
17. *Memorable Characteristics*, in *Select Biographies*, Wodrow Society, vol. 1, p. 347.
18. LSR 292, pp. 545–7.
19. *Memorable Characteristics*, p. 347.
20. LSR 292, p. 547.
21. Ibid.
22. Bonar's Introduction to LSR 311, p. 623.
23. LSR 311, p. 623.
24. LSR 311, p. 624.
25. LSR 314, p. 628.
26. Ibid.
27. LSR 312, pp. 625–6.

CHAPTER 12

1. *Memorable Characteristics*, in *Select Biographies*, Wodrow Society, vol. 1, 1845, p. 361.
2. *The Life of John Livingstone*, in *Select Biographies*, vol. 1, p. 130.
3. Ibid., p. 135.
4. Ibid., p. 194.

5. *Memorable Characteristics*, p. 346.
6. Robert Fleming, *Fulfilling of the Scriptures*. Quoted by John Gillies, *Historical Collections of Accounts of Revival*, Banner of Truth Trust, 1981, p. 198.
7. *Memorable Characteristics*, p. 358.
8. Ibid., p. 363.
9. James Anderson, *The Ladies of the Covenant*, 1862, p. 32.
10. LSR 62, p. 140.
11. LSR 74, p. 157.
12. Ibid.
13. *Memorable Characteristics*, p. 362.
14. LSR 222, p. 433.
15. Ibid., p. 432.
16. LSR 178, p. 337.
17. LSR 90, p. 192.
18. Ibid.
19. *The Letters of John Livingstone*, in *Select Biographies*, vol. 1, p. 263.
20. *Memorable Characteristics*, p. 320.
21. John Howie, *The Scots Worthies*, p. 305.
22. *Memorable Characteristics*, p. 362.

CHAPTER 13

1. John Howie, *The Scots Worthies*, p. 260.
2. LSR 269, p. 521.
3. John Howie, op. cit., p. 265.
4. LSR 330, p. 653.
5. Ibid.
6. LSR 319, p. 636.
7. Ibid.
8. Ibid., p. 637.
9. John Howie, op. cit., p. 216.
10. LSR 357, p. 693.
11. John Howie, op. cit., p. 221.
12. R. M'Ward's Preface to *Joshua Redivivus; or Mr Rutherford's Letters*, 1664.
13. LSR 362, p. 701.
14. LSR 362, p. 702.

CHAPTER 14

1. Patrick Walker, *Lives of Semple, Welwood and Cameron*, 1727, p. 46.
2. Patrick Walker, *Six Saints of the Covenant* (ed. D. Hay Fleming, 1901, pp. 235–6).

3. John Howie, *The Scots Worthies*, p. 186.
4. Ibid., p. 200.
5. Amos 3:2.
6. John Howie, op. cit., p. 382.
7. LSR 362, p. 702.
8. James Anderson, *The Ladies of the Covenant*, 1862, Appendix No. 1, p. 607.
9. John Howie, op. cit., p. 332.
10. John Row, *The History of the Kirk of Scotland from the year 1558 to 1637*, Wodrow Society, 1842, p. 396.
11. LSR 277, p. 536.
12. R.M'Ward's Preface to *Joshua Redivivus; or Mr Rutherford's Letters*, 1664.
13. James Anderson, op. cit., p. 70.
14. Ibid., p. 73.
15. Quoted by Maurice Grant, *No King but Christ*, Evangelical Press, 1988, p. 252.
16. LSR 221, p. 431.
17. Maurice Grant, op. cit., p. 262.

CONCLUSION

1. *Memoirs of the Rev. Thomas Halyburton*, 1849, p. 296.
2. *The Works of the Rev. John Wesley, A.M.*, 1854, p. 127.
3. Josiah Pratt, *Remains of Rev. Richard Cecil*, 1854, p. 284.
4. *Memoirs and Remains of Rev. R.M.M'Cheyne*, 1892, p. 172.
5. Ibid., p. 132.
6. *Andrew Bonar, Diary and Life*, Banner of Truth Trust, 1960, p. 374.
7. C.H. Spurgeon, *The Sword and Trowel*, June 1891.
8. Dr and Mrs Howard Taylor, *Hudson Taylor, The Growth of a Work of God*, 1919, p. 163.
9. Wilbur M. Smith, *Before I Forget*, 1971, p. 196.
10. Jock Purves, *Fair Sunshine*, Banner of Truth Trust, 1968, p. 144.

GRACE IN WINTER

Rutherford in Verse

Faith Cook

By any standard, Samuel Rutherford was a remarkable Christian: as a pastor he was devoted to his congregation in Anwoth, Scotland; as a leading churchman he was selected in 1643 as a member of the Scottish delegation to the famous Westminster Assembly; as a scholar he was offered some of the most distinguished professorships in Europe; as a letter writer Samuel Rutherford stands second to none in the galaxy of those whose personal correspondence has appeared in published form.

Yet, perhaps the description which would have most encouraged and humbled Rutherford himself came from the lips of a visiting Englishman who said of him that he 'heard a little fair man, and he showed me the loveliness of Christ'.

Rutherford knew that the heart of Christian experience is in union and communion with Christ. He saw, with the apostle Paul, that only those who share in the fellowship of Christ's sufferings experience the power of his resurrection. To him, joy in the Lord and suffering for him were inseparable elements of Christian experience. 'Grace' he wrote out of deep personal experience, 'grows best in winter'.

In these pages, Faith Cook has sensitively transformed Rutherford's eloquent prose into the form of poetry, and provided cameo portraits of his correspondents. *Grace in Winter* not only gives pleasure and joy because of its poetry; it also shares the encouragement, comfort and wisdom of Rutherford's own ministry.

Faith Cook, daughter of O.M.F. missionaries, lives in Hull, where her husband Paul is minister of Kingston Reformed Church.

ISBN 0 85151 555 X
96pp. Cloth-bound.

LETTERS OF SAMUEL RUTHERFORD

Selected by Andrew A. Bonar

'What a wealth of spiritual ravishment we have here! Rutherford is beyond all praise of men. Like a strong-winged eagle he soars into the highest heaven and with unblenched eye he looks into the mystery of love divine. There is, to us, something mysterious, awe-creating and superhuman about Rutherford's letters.

'This edition is a noble volume, and we shall measure the soundness of Scotch religion very much by the sale of this work. One page of Rutherford is worth a thousand tomes of the Downgrade frothiness.

'We think it meet to take a paragraph from Dr Andrew Bonar's prefatory sketch:

"The extravagence in sentiment alleged against them by some is that of Paul, when he spoke of knowing 'the height and depth, length and breadth' of the love of Christ: or that of Solomon when the Holy Ghost inspired him to write 'The Song of Songs'. Rather would we say of these letters what John Livingstone, in a letter, says of John Welsh's dying words: 'O for a sweet fill of this fantastic humour!' In modern days Richard Cecil has said of Rutherford, 'He is one of my classics; he is a real original'; and in older times, Richard Baxter, some of whose theological leanings might have prejudiced him, if anything could, said of his letters, 'Hold off the Bible, such a book the world never saw'."

'When we are dead and gone let the world know that Spurgeon held Rutherford's letters to be the nearest thing to inspiration which can be found in all the writings of mere men.'

C. H. Spurgeon in *The Sword and Trowel, 1891.*

ISBN 0 85151 388 3
768pp. Cloth-bound.

For free illustrated catalogue please write to
THE BANNER OF TRUTH TRUST
3 Murrayfield Road, Edinburgh, EH12 6EL
PO Box 621, Carlisle, Pennsylvania 17013, USA